GETTING A ROOF
OVER YOUR HEAD

Compiled by the editors at Garden Way

 GARDEN WAY PUBLISHING, CHARLOTTE, VT 05445

Printed in the United States.

Library of Congress Cataloging in Publication Data
Main entry under title:

Getting a roof over your head.

  Includes index.
  1. House construction— Amateurs' manuals.   2. Building
— Amateurs' manuals.   3. Dwellings— Amateurs' manuals.
I. Garden Way Publishing.
TH4815.G47   1982   690'.837   82-20941
ISBN 0-88266-245-7

Contents

Preface

It's easy to prove you simply can't build or buy your own home.

Look at interest rates, the cost of materials, the price tags on existing homes, the price of land, the big monthly payments.

It's impossible. People, thousands of them, agree with this, and they have given up hope they'll ever own their own homes.

And yet. . . .

And yet thousands more are moving into new homes, and many of them are doing it free of the yoke of a large monthly mortgage payment.

Those of us who wrote this book had no difficulty in finding success stories. And we learned something from each story we wrote. We learned, in general, how they did it.

We found these homeowners shared an all-consuming urge to own their own homes. Getting a roof—a roof they owned—over their heads was tops on their priority lists. They were willing to give up pleasures so they could work on their houses; money that could have gone for restaurant meals or travel was spent on 2x4s and insulation. They had a single goal—and you'd better get out of their way if you're blocking their progress.

Another thing, they had studied their own situations. They realized they had strong points, assets, and wisely they capitalized on them. Those strong points varied, from a nest egg to a building lot, from know-how to time to learn, from parents who would lend a bit of money to the determination to work long hours, day after day, and each time at the end of a day of work on a regular job.

This book is not written to tell of their successes. It is written for you, who may think owning a house is impossible. Read these chapters and relate to them. What's your strong point? How can you capitalize on it, build on it until you have your own home?

It is a book to make you think. You'll find yourself saying, "I could do that too. And if I did, then I could. . . ."

And you'll be on your way to finding the home you only dream about today.

Roland Wells Robbins's reproduction of the Thoreau house.

LEARN FROM THOREAU

Building the house you want for the amount you want to spend.

In March 1845, Henry David Thoreau borrowed an axe and began building his house near Walden Pond, not far from his home in Concord, Massachusetts.

He moved in on July 4, and lived there alone until September 6, 1847. During those two years and two months he wrote the journals that later he would expand into *Walden,* a lively classic on how to live fully and simply.

Thoreau's *Walden* is still timely to those who seek an alternative to the frantic materialism of modern living.

It's timely, too, to those of us who long to build a home, but see no way over the lofty obstacles of monthly payments, interest rates, and costs of materials. Thoreau tells exactly how he cut costs. He wanted to demonstrate that he could build a house and not pay for it and for the borrowed money for the rest of his days, as so many of his neighbors in Concord did.

Scholars may object to such a homely use of the words of this poet-naturalist-philosopher, a use that suggests that *Walden* is in part a how-to book on inexpensive housing. Thoreau wouldn't object. He was a practical man. He wanted his words to be used by those learning to spend less time in providing themselves with food, clothing, and shelter, learning to live better.

Rules on Building

Here are some of the rules on building that Thoreau suggests.

Build small. Those of us planning to build, and hoping to build efficiently, can save thousands of dollars by acting on Thoreau's advice on planning a house: "Consider first how slight a shelter is absolutely necessary."

Thoreau's decision for his house: one room ten by fifteen feet, a garret reached by a trapdoor, and a closet. A fireplace, and later a small cookstove. Outside, a small woodshed. Under the house, a root cellar. This house offered a place for his bed, his writing table, a few tools and utensils, and storage space for fuel and food. No running water—the water of Walden Pond was nearby. No extra rooms to impress visitors. No

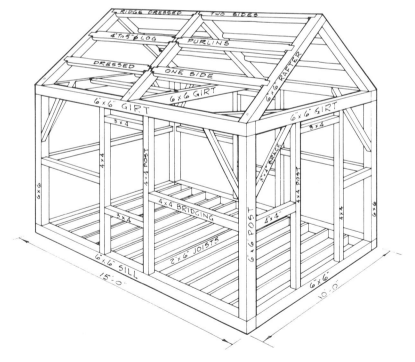

The framework of the Thoreau house.

By Roger M. Griffith

1

> **"I went to the woods because I wished to live deliberately, to front only the essential facts of life, and see if I could not learn what it had to teach, and not, when I came to die, discover that I had not lived."**
>
> **Thoreau**

Thoreau salvaged bricks for a chimney like this.

space to store things that weren't necessary; those would only clutter both the home and his life.

Avoid a mortgage if possible. Because his home was modest and he built it, there was no need for Thoreau to "hire" mortgage money from a bank. He warned against borrowing, fearing that soon, instead of the house serving him, he would be working for it to pay for it.

It was time to build. "Near the end of March, 1845, I borrowed an axe and went down to the woods by Walden Pond, nearest to where I intended to build my house, and began to cut down some tall, arrowy white pines, still in their youth, for timber."

In that sentence Thoreau offered several pointers for the would-be builder, as a way to save both money and work.

Do as much of your own work as you can. This can cut building costs as much as 25 percent.

Don't spend on tools if you can avoid it. Borrow them. Thoreau explained it this way: "It is difficult to begin without borrowing, but perhaps it is the most generous course thus to permit your fellow-men to have an interest in your enterprise."

And be a good borrower, as Thoreau believed he was when he borrowed that axe. "The owner of the axe, as he released his hold on it, said that it was the apple of his eye; but I returned it sharper than I received it."

Use native materials that are handy. He used the pines of Walden woods for all his timbers.

2

View from the Robbins house.

"If you have built castles in the air, your work need not be lost; that is where they should be. Now put the foundations under them."

Thoreau

Thoreau now had the timbers for the framework of his house. He needed much more—boards for the sides of the house, two windows, a door, other materials. His method is still timely.

Use salvaged materials. An Irish railroad worker lived in a shanty nearby. Thoreau bought it for $4.25, took it apart carefully, even saving the nails and spikes (which were stolen before he could use them), then moved all by small cartloads to his site.

Get volunteer help. It was time to raise the framework. Thoreau never considered hiring help for this heavy work. It just wasn't done that way. He saw it as an "occasion for neighborliness" and assembled his acquaintances to pull and push, haul and hold firm, fit and

Select those materials carefully. By selecting tall pines, Thoreau reduced the number he had to fell. By selecting slim pines, all in their youth, he had timbers that needed little cutting or shaping, thus cutting the amount of axe work.

Thoreau described how he shaped the pine logs. "I hewed the main timbers six inches square, most of the studs on two sides only, and the rafters and floor timbers on one side, leaving the rest of the bark on, so that they were just as straight and much stronger than sawed ones. Each stick was carefully mortised or tenoned by its stump, for I had borrowed other tools by this time." He did his work carefully, but wasted no time or effort hewing all sides of studs or rafters, or peeling off bark.

> "I learned this, at least, by my experiment: that if one advances confidently in the direction of his dreams, and endeavors to live the life which he has imagined, he will meet with a success unexpected in common hours."
> **Thoreau**

pound, and finally stand back and admire how it all fitted together so firm and so true.

Build a root cellar. It costs so little, and can mean great savings in food bills. Thoreau's was under his house, reached by a trap door, and was six feet square by seven feet deep. "It was but two hours' work," he wrote.

When he moved in, the house wasn't completed. There was a gaping hole where there would be a chimney, and the boards weren't shingled over. Thoreau was confident he could finish the house before the cold of winter—and he did.

Move in—When?

There's many an argument about the wisdom of moving into a house before it is finished. Pro-movers say you can cut costs, particularly if you're renting until your house is completed. They say, too, that you're right at work—even surrounded by it—if you move in. If you're short on money, you can finish the house as money becomes available.

Anti-movers say it takes longer if you move in. It's just too easy to let up, to get accustomed to the unhung door of the bathroom, the two sawhorses in the living room, and not to notice that nothing is getting done until you see your home in all its disarray through the startled eyes of a visitor, come to admire your beautiful new house.

You, the builder, must decide. How strong is your character? How determined are you to get the job done?

Thoreau built the chimney—with used bricks—shingled the exterior, plastered the interior, then admired his tidy home. He was proud of the work, joking, "I intend to build me a house which will surpass any on the main street in Concord in grandeur and luxury, as soon as it pleases me as much and will cost me no more than my present one."

He built this one for $28.12½.

And built it with his own hands, if not his own tools.

May you do as well with your house. A reading of *Walden* is sure to help.

A Reproduction of Thoreau's Cabin

The Depression of the Thirties cut short Roland Wells Robbins's education in mid-high school. Since then he's been self-taught. He's majored in the writings of Thoreau. He has studied the man, his life, and his writings, so thoroughly that today it's difficult to distinguish when Roland Wells Robbins is speaking, or when he is quoting Thoreau. A tendency to emphasize the first

THOREAU'S LIST OF EXPENSES AS LISTED IN *WALDEN*

Boards	$8 03½,	mostly shanty boards.
Refuse shingles for roof and sides	4 00	
Laths	1 25	
Two second-hand windows with glass	2 43	
One thousand old brick	4 00	
Two casks of lime	2 40	That was high.
Hair	0 31	More than I needed
Mantle-tree iron	0 15	
Nails	3 90	
Hinges and screws	0 14	
Latch	0 10	
Chalk	0 01	
Transportation	1 40	I carried a good part on my back
	$28 12½	

4

5

The home, the woodshed — and the borrowed axe.

word in quotations gives the listener a hint as to whether Robbins or Thoreau is speaking.

Robbins is credited with pinpointing the location of Thoreau's house on the shores of Walden Pond. While the modest house lives vividly in the minds of all who have read *Walden*, the actual building was moved several times, then finally torn apart, and the boards used in the construction of a Concord barn. The exact location of the cabin was long forgotten.

Robbins attended the 100th anniversary celebration of Thoreau's moving into his home, a gathering of literary folks held at Walden Pond on July 4, 1945. He

was challenged by the speaker of the day, historian Allen French of Concord, to locate the exact site of the house, a subject of much concern at that centennial celebration.

And find it he did, after much probing of both Thoreau's writing and, with a steel rod, the soil around Walden Pond.

This led Robbins into a new career, from housecleaning and window washing to historical archeologist, or "pick-and-shovel historian," as an article in *Collier's* magazine in 1955 called him.

His work has included important historical finds in such areas as Thomas Jefferson's birthplace

in Virginia, the 1646 Saugus, Massachusetts, Iron Works, and the 1627 John Alden Home.

It finally led him back to Thoreau and his house. Robbins and his wife live on a spacious, wooded lot in Lincoln, Massachusetts, and there, in 1964, he duplicated, as accurately as he could, the Thoreau house.

The house sits up on a slight rise, in a clump of trees, isolated from the other buildings on the lot. Inside it is simply furnished. Outside there's a privy and a woodshed. There's a door on the front of the house, one window on each of the side walls, and a fireplace on the rear wall.

Robbins generously permits

Roland Wells Robbins

lacks, or more probably because of them, the house offers a big plus, a feeling of calmness, quiet, and serenity, a place to reflect and think. It's a place, as Thoreau said, "to live deliberately, to front only the essential facts of life. . . ."

Encouraged by the enthusiasm with which the memorial cabin was greeted, Robbins arranged for the sale of a kit, to include the pine frame, but not materials that could be bought (or scavenged, as Thoreau did) locally. The kit sells for $3,856 plus shipping. Write to House of Thoreau, P.O. Box 91, Concord, MA 01742, for free material.

visitors to stay for a few hours or even a night in the Thoreau house, and those who have stayed include honeymooners, an Indian high court justice, folk singers—and hundreds of Thoreau fans.

Most of them have reported a curious reaction—that the minuses of the little house add up to a huge plus. The minuses are the lacks of the house, which doesn't have electricity, running water, television, radios, or many other things most of us think of as necessities. Despite these

THINK AHEAD

Planning can mean lower maintenance costs.

At first glance, it bears a striking resemblance to a World War II bunker, hunkered into the ground to withstand the enemy's next assault. But in the energy-conserving community of Village Homes in Davis, California, the only war is the battle against high energy costs and steep housing prices.

The latest recruit is a youthful architect who's styled his unconventional home to beat high prices on two fronts: in initial construction and later when paying utility bills.

Low Maintenance Costs

Jim Zanetto, who spent nearly $30,000 to build his family's earth-sheltered home three years ago, says constructing it themselves was the only way they could afford to jump into the housing market. And stay there. By snuggling their two-bedroom into the ground for insulation and by relying largely on the sun for heating and on nighttime breezes for cooling, the Zanettos pay virtually nothing in utility bills. "It allows us to get by on less because the house doesn't require a lot of income to maintain," notes the 34-year-old architect happily.

But for the Zanetto family—Jim, his wife, Donna, and their

By Claudia Buck

nine-year-old son, Aaron—building their own home was as much an economic necessity as a personal challenge. "It was something we really wanted to do," says Jim, perched on a stool in his architectural studio, a small stark office papered with blueprints and renderings, just off the living room.

"We wanted to try some techniques that would have been fairly expensive if we hadn't done it ourselves," says Zanetto, who hired his brother Jeff to help erect the innovative structure. He figures they trimmed about $5,000 off the price by hammering it together themselves. "We had very littly money to begin with," notes Donna, "and just bringing it down those few thousand dollars helped."

What they wound up with is unconventional on today's housing menu—a home that's dug into the ground, using the earth as a natural heat blanket. It's estimated by the Underground Space Center at the University of Minnesota, the country's clearinghouse on underground housing, that somewhere between 3,000 and 5,000 underground homes had been built by 1980. That's not particularly remarkable, unless you consider that two years before, the American Institute of Architects estimated that only thirty or forty underground homes existed

in the country. If those numbers are accurate, the jump from 30 to 3,000 in two years is remarkable, an indication that homeowners are looking for innovative ways to keep their energy costs down. It's estimated that earth-sheltered homes use 25 to 80 percent less energy than conventional houses of comparable size. What's more, say earth-sheltered homeowners, the houses are quieter, less likely to be attacked by termites and dry-rot, usually more fire-resistant, and generally safer from high winds or severe storms.

Energy Savings

Zanetto went underground primarily because of the energy savings. By packing the walls with 45° banks of earth and planting the roof with eight inches of dirt, Zanetto says the house is enveloped "in a real benign temperature medium." All that dirt—ten feet deep at the sides—shields the compact residence from fluctuations in outdoor temperatures, which can play havoc in heating and cooling a conventional home.

"It's a passive solar house first and an underground home second," says Zanetto, a University of Southern California architecture graduate. Actually, he prefers to describe it as an "earth-sheltered" dwelling, which bet-

Jim, Aaron, and Donna Zanetto.

ter explains the sloping wings of packed dirt that mound up the east and west sides of the one-story home and continue across the planted rooftop. Along the back of the home, which faces north onto a community green-belt of fruit trees and vegetable gardens, the earth is cut away for a sunken private courtyard that opens off the two bedrooms.

Earth Is Warm

According to Zanetto, who combed libraries for the scant materials available on underground architecture when he launched his housebuilding project, the earth's temperature ten feet deep hovers between 60° and 70° year-round in his area. This provides a stable barrier that protects the house from temperature swings in the outside air.

And while earth is a poor insulator, it's an ideal source of mass, reducing summer heat gain and winter heat loss. Whereas a conventional home will lose great amounts of heat through the walls and roof (unless they're heavily insulated), an earth-bermed house is largely oblivious to outside changes in weather. In summer, the house loses heat to the cool earth, rather than gaining heat from the surrounding air; in winter, the relatively warm soil locks in heat. For the Zanettos, it means they derive approximately 80 percent of their heating and 100 percent of their air conditioning from the house itself.

Problem Is Cooling

In Davis, a university town 15 miles west of Sacramento, California's capital, the mercury often climbs over the 100° mark in summer. Cooling, consequently, is a more crucial concern than heating. Summer is also the time of peak electrical use in this climate due to air conditioning. The construction of new power plants, whose per-unit costs are much higher than the costs from existing power plants, can be minimized by a

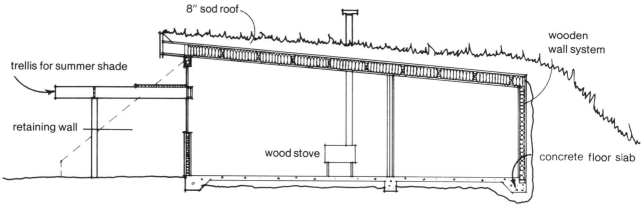

8″ sod roof

wooden wall system

trellis for summer shade

retaining wall

wood stove

concrete floor slab

A blanket of earth surrounds all but one side of this house.

By reducing their utility bills, the Zanettos have, in essence, purchased insurance against the upward spiral of gas and electricity rates.

wider use of natural cooling strategies.

The Zanettos, despite a full wall of heat-soaking, south-facing windows but not a single piece of mechanical air conditioning, report they stay cool as cucumbers throughout Davis's sizzling summers. During a ten-day spell of stifling temperatures, when the thermometer soared above 100° every day, the earth berms stayed a pleasant 70° while temperatures inside the house never topped 82°, notes the homeowner. (To monitor temperatures, Zanetto has thirty-five sensors imbedded in the berms, roof, walls, and slab floor.)

On summer evenings, the Zanettos rely on cool, night breezes to flush hot air out of the house. There are no fans, no exterior shades, and no air conditioning. But there are lots of operable windows. The house is ideally situated for natural cooling, located across from a heavily irrigated playing field, a vast expanse of cool, green grass that offers no barriers to breezes that blow in from the Carquinez Straits.

Drapes Help

Although they worried that without exterior shading across their bank of south-facing windows they'd roast in the summers, it hasn't proved to be a problem. The windows are doubled-paned and Donna stitched together foil-lined interior drapes which the couple draws across the windows on summer days to keep the heat out. They plan on installing shades in an effort to keep peak interior temperatures in the 70's.

For the Zanettos, natural cooling means double the savings: construction was easier, faster, and cheaper because there was no air-conditioning equipment to install, and they save every time they don't have to flip the switch for cooling.

As for keeping warm, the family's only "manmade" heat source is a small, black wood-burning stove. On cozy winter evenings, it's the focal point of the living area.

The house itself also acts as a heat source, with the uncovered concrete slab floor, a thermal mass, soaking up winter sun and

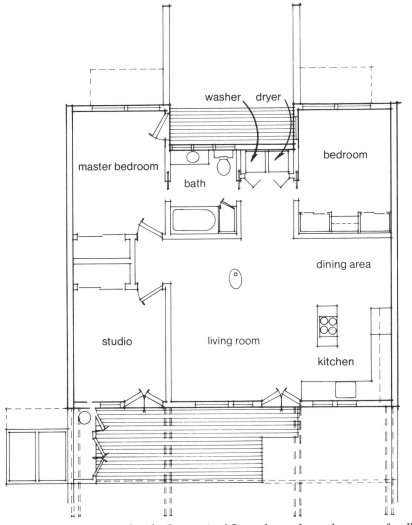

Dotted lines on south side (bottom) of floor plan indicate location of trellis.

Labels in floor plan: washer, dryer, master bedroom, bath, bedroom, dining area, studio, living room, kitchen

an insulating blanket of earth, he was able to retain the heat captured in the concrete floor—without the need for water-filled columns, bulky concrete additions, or windows piercing the sod roof.

Never Cold

The coldest it's ever been indoors is 60°. "We build a fire when it gets down to about 65° or 66° and it warms up the whole house right away," explains Donna, an elementary school secretary.

Solar, and especially earth-sheltered buildings, often have relatively comfortable "radiant temperatures" on their walls, floors, and ceilings. This allows occupants to be comfortable at air temperatures that could not be acceptable in more conventional structures.

Because of the home's thermally blanketed design, the Zanettos pay nothing for air conditioning and only what it costs to keep the woodstove filled for heating. And that's been essentially zero, since they burn scrap wood, initially collected from

radiating that warmth back into the house at night. Concerned that the concrete might not soak up enough warmth, Zanetto and his brother poured extra-thick footings below the south-facing windows to support a row of water-filled drums. They've never been needed.

In Zanetto's mind, that's one of the virtues of underground homes versus well-designed passive solar homes. "The limitation of a passive solar house is that it requires a large amount of ther-

mal mass and that becomes more expensive as the house gets larger. Plus, you need that mass, either in water (columns or culverts) or .nasonry, in front of your south-facing windows and that blocks a lot of your view."

Also in order to slip winter sunlight into the northern regions of the house, many passive solar homes rely on clerestory windows or skylights. With a sod roof, Zanetto wanted neither intrusion.

By enveloping his home with

11

their own site and lately gathered from a free community stockpile of construction leftovers in Village Homes. "We really think we're going to be able to continue doing that because society is so wasteful. So much wood is just thrown away," remarked the spare, soft-spoken architect.

Consequently, the family's utility bills are agreeably low—never exceeding $20 a month for a gas stove, dryer, washing machine, and gas water heater. That's part of the home's long-range savings. By reducing their utility bills, the Zanettos have, in essence, purchased insurance against the upward spiral of gas and electricity rates. At a time when many homeowners find themselves facing utility bills larger than their mortgage payments, the Zanettos are largely oblivious to the whims of OPEC.

"The solution is not to fight whoever's charging you the bill, but to find a living solution that uses less energy," states Zanetto, who's designing other underground homes for California clients. "When people are paying $500 a month just to stay comfortable, they've got a tremendous opportunity (and incentive) to finance energy-conservation devices (more so) than when they were paying only $50 a month for utilities."

Didn't Go Solar

Ironically, that kind of economic equation is why this energy-conscious family has postponed its original plan to install a solar water heating system. A glassed-in "breadbox" solar

Jim Zanetto: "Society is so wasteful."

water heater, sunk into a bank of insulating earth on the home's west flank, sits ready but empty. "It'd cost us about $300 to get a solar system installed," figures Zanetto, "but it only costs us about $5 a month to heat our water with gas so it's not a high priority. When it gets to $10 or $15 a month, we'll consider solar water heating."

They also save on electricity by relying on natural lighting. "Most people have the idea that it's dark (in an underground home). They think we're moles living in a kind of hole," laughs Donna, freckled and wholesome looking. "But we've got one of the most naturally lit homes in the village—in all of Davis. Even on dark days, we don't need all the lights on."

Good Natural Light

Far from being cave-like, the home's narrow depth means there aren't any rooms deprived of windows. The bank of south-facing glass across the front of the house illuminates (and warms) the family's main activity center. Along the back of the house, which looks north, the bedrooms are lit with "light shelves," white-painted extensions off the windows, designed to bounce light into the room off the ceiling. The bright square of light on the bedroom ceilings indicates how well the light shelves are performing.

Skylight Not Needed

Nevertheless, in a last-minute bout of nervousness that there wouldn't be enough light, Zanetto added a skylight in the hallway separating the two bedrooms—but now feels it wasn't necessary. Even though there's not a single pane of glass piercing through the thick, earth-bound walls on east and west,

Interior of earth-sheltered house need not be dark and dreary.

Zanetto says his home boasts as much glass as a similar-sized conventional home.

The Zanettos tackled home-building with a minimum of construction experience. As an architect, Jim had some familiarity with how a house goes together. And he'd spent a few weekends and several summers pounding nails for friends and on construction crews. Except for the electrical, plumbing, Sheetrock, and finishing the slab, he and his brother did all the construction.

Donna painted, sewed the insulated drapes, and nailed up plywood.

Enjoyable Experience

Three years later, Zanetto looks back on the experience fondly. "My brother helped me and it became a real family project. Before we started, people were always telling us, 'You'll look back on this and wish you'd never started.' I always had that in the back of my mind

but it never really happened with us."

That's partly because Zanetto planned every step in meticulous detail. "We had very detailed drawings and tried to anticipate most problems and work them out in advance. It really pays to think things out before you have a pile of wood standing there in front of you." In the case of the home's north-facing windows, tightly tucked into their berth of earth, every step was mapped out on paper before the brothers

ever hit dirt. When it came time to carve the windows out of the earth, they simply followed their paper guidelines step by step.

"It was designed to be built by a non-professional builder," explains Zanetto. "The house is really simple and straightforward. It paid off because it allowed us to work quickly. And the detailing wasn't that difficult because we kept everything simple. If we'd made it any larger, it would've been harder."

They finished the basics in eight months, although when the family moved in, everything wasn't in place; no kitchen cabinets or appliances, no doorknobs, no curtains. They cooked on a hot plate and slept amid the construction chaos.

Get Experience

Zanetto recommends anyone thinking of tackling housebuilding to find someone—a friend, neighbor, relative—starting a similar project and pitch in. "Get in on a housebuilding project as early as you can, right from the drawing stages, so you can get a feel for what's involved. It'll hone skills you might not realize you have."

He also recommended scouting around early for the best subcontractors. "Do it well in advance. Know who the best ones are in your area so you don't start looking in the Yellow Pages the day it's time to start putting in the plumbing."

Zanetto and his brother hired subcontractors for the plumbing and electrical work because they didn't feel competent enough. They hired installers to insulate and Sheetrock the walls and ceilings because "we didn't want to handle the insulation material and we felt that professionals can do it a whole lot faster." And although he and his brother hammered together the wooden forms and poured the concrete, they brought in subs to finish the slab. "It was August and real hot weather," recalls Zanetto, "so there wasn't much room for ex-

14

perimenting. We wanted to get it right the first time."

Above all, Zanetto says, don't be afraid to lean on your local building department. "Most people set up an adversary role with their building department," notes the architect, "but you can use it for advice—and get it right over the telephone."

Asked Experts

That was a pattern he followed throughout construction: asking experts when he was uncertain about a particular step, whether it was a landscaper for the right type of ground cover or a structural engineer on how much support the dirt-packed roof required.

One of their major expenses was $2,000 to hire the developer of Village Homes—Michael Corbett, who's earned worldwide acclaim for his energy-saving subdivision—to guide them through the project. Corbett arranged the financing, scheduled the subcontractors, and showered them with advice. "His foreman was always available for advice," Zanetto gratefully recalls, "with answers for our questions, like, 'How tall do you frame a doorway?'"

In addition, Corbett had stockpiled a cache of leftover building materials from other sites, which were available to the Zanettos as residents of Village Homes. "It saved us a lot of time," recalls the homebuilder. "Instead of driving downtown every time we needed an extra 2x4, it was right there."

When he originally thought of building an earth-sheltered home, Zanetto worried that it might look shrunken and puny beside the many tall, solar two-stories sprinkled throughout the subdivision. Instead, he and Corbett decided to group three earth-covered dwellings (another single-family home and a duplex) in a row facing the neighborhood's community green, where kids fly kites, dogs romp, and neighbors stroll. Although nestled amid a trio of earth-sheltered homes, the Zanetto residence is the most extensively blanketed with dirt and vegetation.

That was by design. One of Zanetto's motivations in creating an underground home was to improve its aesthetics. "We just wanted to see what sort of form could be developed—a planted landscape instead of a typical house form" noted Jim. "And we wanted to see how it would integrate in a moderate-density cluster where the whole neighborhood density is only three units per acre."

Basic Technologies

Nevertheless, he doesn't consider his home experimental, merely an architect's tinkering with a new toy. "We didn't try anything that hadn't been done before. It was basically assembling some basic technologies. People have been building basements for hundreds of years and this is just an extension of that."

Nevertheless, construction involved some unique techniques. Zanetto erected the 1,025-square-foot house out of treated wood. To seal out moisture, the entire framework was draped top-to-bottom in a synthetic rubber material called Hypalon, originally developed as a pond liner. In the process of searching for a supplier, Zanetto carried his working drawings to the manufacturer, who subsequently dispatched two installers to help drape the rubber material over the house's skeleton.

Despite the professional help, they made one mistake: not protecting the Hypalon from punctures. Even though it's buried under eight inches of soil, the rubbery material failed to escape the sharp points of gardening tools. "After the first winter without any leaks, the next

On summer evenings, the Zanettos rely on cool, night breezes to flush hot air out of the house. There are no fans, no exterior shades, and no air conditioning. But there are lots of operable windows.

planting season we were poking around and literally poked holes in it. We found the leaks that next winter," Jim ruefully recalls. "It would have been so easy to lay down a layer of rigid insulation over the Hypalon when we were building. It's all a matter of planning ahead."

Layer of Drainage

The other "significantly unusual" feature in constructing the home was a foot-thick wrap of gravel that was backfilled against all exterior walls up to the roofline. Designed for drainage, the gravel was set in before the dirt was packed around the structure. Sandwiching it between the house and a cloth drainage mesh used in highway construction was the most time-consuming part of the job.

To prevent the home's earthen exterior from becoming a mudslide in the rain or blowing away in a windstorm, the sides and roof are heavily planted. "We put in three times as much landscaping as a typical house," claims Zanetto, who seeded the ground with a variety of low-maintenance, drought-tolerant plants and shrubs.

Bought Cuttings

Because plants were such a major part of the project, the couple hired a landscaping consultant. To cut corners, they purchased tiny cuttings at half the cost of leafy, mature plants. "They come on slow but when you have this much area to cover, it's the only reasonable way to go," explains Zanetto,

who has a master's degree in landscape architecture and environmental planning from the University of California in Berkeley.

The roof is sprinkled with strawberry plants, baccharis, native aster, scabiosa, and myoporum, which are watered from a spigot poking through the roof. To keep weeds down and watering efficient, the berms are mulched with straw.

The original idea to landscape the roof with bunch grass was abandoned because the native plants turn brown in summer. "We wanted plants that would stay green all year," explains Jim, "and we wanted a variety because we thought it might be a difficult place to grow things."

There's a pathway planned across the rooftop, which is structurally sturdy enough to hike around on. On balmy summer evenings, it's an ideal spot for watching sunsets.

Because of that, Zanetto sees the vegetation as a boon for his neighbors, as well. "It's fairly dense housing here and this is an attempt to relieve that. Your view is not so much another house but a planted landscape."

Edible Landscaping

Out front, the landscaping is edible. Since the Zanettos' house fronts on a lush playing field, they felt there was no need for another green lawn. Instead, they substituted it with a winter

Jim Zanetto explains financing techniques.

garden of lettuce, broccoli, onions, Swiss chard, cabbage, fava beans, brussels sprouts, and radishes.

The six-foot-deep backyard is filled with ornamental plants that spill onto a community garden, a plot shared and communally gardened by the Zanettos and their five neighbors. The backyard is small by choice. The Zanettos purposely pushed the house as far north on the lot as possible to maximize the sunny front yard for gardening and solar gain through their front windows. "With the common area behind us, we don't feel that it's private property (butting up) against us."

One Mistake

What mistakes did they make in building themselves? Zanetto doesn't hesitate. "Coming to the end of your construction budget and realizing there's a lot you'd still like to do. That's the most mentally stressful part of building for yourself." Their biggest regret is that they didn't add in the cost of tiling the floors, which still are naked concrete. They'll be finished as time—and money—permit.

Financing proved to be one of the trickiest parts of building. The Zanettos' goal was to keep their monthly payments as low as possible. "If you're trying to stay on a low budget, calculate the loan very carefully," advises Zanetto. "Every $1,000 we borrowed was $10 more on our monthly payment." (It's significantly more if interest rates are higher.)

To keep that amount low, they

ROUGH COST BREAKDOWN, ZANETTO HOUSE (± 80% OWNER BUILT)

Plans (by owner)	$ 0
Building permit	1450
Earthwork*	900
Concrete**	3400
Lumber	6350
Moisture proof membrane**	1800
Windows	2575
Doors	850
Carpentry labor	1900
Electric*	1500
Plumbing*	2500
Sheetrock*	1950
Cabinets	400
Heating/air conditioning	0
Wood stove	300
Insulation*	700
Misc.	1000
Solar D.H.W. (breadbox)	400
General contractor	2000
Total	$29,975

* = subcontractor
** = part subcontractor, part by owner

jettisoned additional sums for redwood decking, solar awnings, floor tile, and landscaping from the mortgage. "You have to decide what you really need to live with now and what you can afford to wait for," said Zanetto.

Paid Back Down Payment

The only sum they borrowed was their down payment— $4,000 borrowed from his parents, which they managed to pay back by the time the house was built. "We got bids for every item in construction," explains Zanetto. "If a bid was $2,000 for the slab floor, then my brother and I had that much budget to work with. If materials cost

more, we got paid less. If not and we worked quickly, we were able to save some of that money." By that technique, they managed to scrape together enough to pay back the down payment by the time the house was completed.

Although they managed to shave off a healthy chunk of money by building themselves, the Zanettos say their greatest motivation was that they wanted to tackle the challenge. "You must have a much greater knowledge of what it's all about. When something doesn't work well, you have an idea why. There's just a more personal involvement with the house."

Try Walking

They also enjoy a more personal involvement with their neighborhood: Village Homes, the sun-drenched community of 200 solar homes that grew up out of seventy acres of tomato fields to become one of the world's models of energy-minded living. As envisioned by Michael and Judy Corbett, Village Homes is oriented away from the automobile and toward energy efficiency. Streets are narrower than the norm (to reduce the summer heat buildup from miles of exposed asphalt), bike paths meander through the development, and most streets end in cul-de-sacs to discourage aimless cruising in cars. It's deliberately easier to walk or bicycle from one end of the subdivision to another than it is to drive.

All the lots face north-south, assuring the homes plenty of solar exposure. To conserve land, the lots are also narrower, front yards are smaller than usual (and usually fenced for privacy), and the backyards (like the Zanettos') run unhindered onto the shared neighborhood greenbelts, where each group of neighbors democratically decides whether to garden, build a playyard, or landscape their shared plot.

That land conservation freed up enough acreage to provide a community center, playing fields, and a fifteen-acre community farm, including orchards, vegetable fields, and a thriving vineyard, whose neatly tailored rows stretch alongside the Zanettos' west flank.

Solar Water Heating

According to the Corbetts, nearly all the homes utilize some type of passive solar design and fewer than 10 percent (among them the Zanettos') don't have solar water heating. It all adds up to some impressive savings: Village Homes residents consume at least 50 percent less gas and electricity than do other Davis homeowners, according to some studies.

Although criticized by some

Aaron Zanetto enjoys life in Village Homes.

for its emphasis on a cooperative lifestyle (besides a shared gardening plot, residents are encouraged to join weekend work parties to help build retaining walls, play areas, a swimming pool complex, bridges, and other features), it still earns high marks and continues to lure hundreds of national and international tourists who come to view its unique approach to neighborhood planning.

Great for Kids

It was the only spot the Zanetto family, who'd been living in a tiny Davis apartment, wanted to live. But it was more than a philosophical attraction. "Aside from being energy efficient, it's just a great place to raise kids," grins Zanetto, as he watches a pair of youthful kite flyers outside his window.

"We consciously stayed away from five-acre places in the hills. Land is a real valuable resource. People should be trying to live in more dense situations. Economics is driving us in that direction very strongly."

Sprawling subdivisions, where residents must drive to reach jobs, shopping, and entertainment, are a burden on society, says Zanetto. They force homeowners to pay more for utilities and services that are strung out ever-longer distances. As neighborhoods inevitably become smaller and denser, so should the homes that fill them, Zanetto believes.

His own home would fit the bill, although at 1,025 square feet it's considered cramped by most standards. It's two bedrooms, one bath, a studio that is Zanetto's architectural office, and a kitchen that melts into the family's main living center, a high-ceilinged room whose dominant feature is the petite woodburning stove.

No Garage

There is no garage. They park their only car beneath a trellis at the end of their cul-de-sac. An enclosed storage space is envisioned for the cul-de-sac. Their washer and dryer are concealed in a utility closet.

"We don't feel cramped at all," assures the architect, although he regrets the house lacks a sewing room and working space for his wife. That might have required more square footage to accomplish, he says, but essentially it would have been a matter of allocating space more efficiently.

"People have images of spaces largely patterned after what they've lived in or have seen. I certainly have that bias. But we should think of what rooms are going to be used for." In the case of a bedroom, for example, he noted that some use it only for sleeping; others utilize it as a home office; others require storage for a "tremendous amount of clothes. In most situations, it could either be made larger to take in more uses as a den or library—or be made smaller to be just a sleeping space."

Zanetto had other ideas for homeowners to keep housing costs cheap. Buying a big chunk of land cooperatively and subdividing it into smaller parcels among a group of buyers is one.

That way, the costs of improvements can be shared while still affording everyone an individual piece of property at a lower cost.

Facilities Shared

Shared facilities such as cooperative laundries is another. "That strikes me as a real primary use that could be shared by families. People in apartments have been doing it a long time. If it's clean, well-maintained, secure, and handy, then people could save a lot by not having to buy a washer and dryer for every home. And you wouldn't have to tie up that part of the house (now used for laundry) and could eliminate the extra plumbing." However, he sheepishly admitted, he didn't initiate the idea in his own neighborhood and the Zanettos do have their own laundry facilities.

But they do share gardening tools with their neighbors. "There's no need for every family to have a complete tool setup. There's so much repetition from one family to another for tools you only use once a year." Zanetto and his neighbors share a lawnmower and wheelbarrow, purchased jointly, that are stored in one resident's garage.

Regardless, Zanetto believes houses of the future will be smaller than the standard tract house of ten or twenty years ago. "It's more energy-efficient in terms of cold, hard numbers (i.e., utility bills and construction costs), but it also makes a more comfortable, pleasant place to live." And Zanetto feels he and his family are living in a perfect example.

TAKE A BUILDER'S COURSE

You'll gain a knowledge of carpentry, a feel for design, and a
better chance of building your dream house.

"From the General Store go a half-mile south on the dirt road up a steep hill; when the road forks, go right for three miles. At the next intersection, take a sharp right up the hill. You'll be on a logging road. Pass by a log cabin on your right, take the left fork. . . ."

The directions to Janet Macleod's home in Adamant, Vermont, keep one shifting in and out of first gear, but at the end of the road in a small clearing sits her 1½-story saltbox. The woodframe house is sited among a mature growth of evergreens with just a hint of the mountains beyond. For the past two years Janet has been designer, contractor, and crew for her owner-built home, still being built.

Janet is a slight, soft-spoken woman in her mid-thirties who has twice built from the ground up. This time she says, "I'm really happy with it. The space has turned out just as I had hoped." She has much to be proud of.

Janet has always had an interest in carpentry, only now it is a more conscious pursuit. "Ever since I can remember," she says, "my family has lived in old houses. Things *always* needed to be shored up, or fixed or patched. You never knew if you were

By Mary Twitchell

doing it 'right' but as long as the nails held you were satisfied. I'm sure I'd be horrified now by some of our makeshift carpentry," she adds with a chuckle.

Built Small Houses

After living in New Hampshire, Massachusetts, and Rhode Island, Janet returned to her home state of Vermont where she works as a member of an energy audit team for the university Extension Service. With the help of an uncle who is a carpenter, she embarked on building her first home—a one-room, one-story, 20×24-foot house.

The experience gave her on-site experience. "My uncle pretty much left me alone," she explains. "I learned by watching him. But whenever he'd see me doing something absurdly wrong, he'd say in his dry Vermont way, 'You'd *perhaps* do it this way.' Although he didn't talk much, I learned a lot; most importantly I developed a sense of confidence."

Owner-Builder Course

Janet's needs soon outgrew the one room, but before she went on to start her present house she attended a fifteen-week course given one evening a week by the director of a local owner-builder school. She had already bought a

fifteen-acre woodlot with the intention of building again.

"The course made me think the whole thing through," she says, "from the dream to the interior detail."

This step-by-step process she has documented in a scrapbook of class assignments and floor plans. It is a very useful planning tool.

The scrapbook begins with professional-looking site plans, drawn to scale, which locate boundaries, ledges, rock outcroppings, water (springs, streams, bogs, ponds), trees (fruit trees, hardwoods, softwoods), views, existing utility lines, topography (or ground slope), existing buildings (including neighbors), existing roads (including town and logging roads), and other natural features. As Janet explains, all these site conditions influence the placement and shape of the house.

Possible Sites

A second plot plan designates five possible house sites with advantages and disadvantages listed for each.

"I checked on the possible sites in both summer and winter. Since there is a bog and thick evergreen growth on the land," she continues, "it was especially important to know the direction of the prevailing winds in case there would be a mosquito problem. I knew noise would be no problem because I am up above the road, but I wasn't sure how the path of the sun, winter storm directions, and the summer run-off would affect each of the spots I had chosen. I also needed information about the views. That was made easier by the hurricane of '73 which felled quite a number of trees (and left a mess on the forest floor)."

Test Borings

Soil composition was another concern. "In the course, we discussed who to contact for soil samples and how to procure soil maps. You don't want to choose a site without researching the subsoil because clay or ledge may run just beneath the surface." Janet spent her weekends traversing all fifteen acres, shovel in hand, making test borings of the soil.

"I also learned about land deeds," she says wryly. "I thought water would be no problem. The land had water; in fact two springs were easily identifiable by the rotting boards around them. Since I owned the land around both springs, I thought it followed that I had the water rights as well." Such

didn't prove to be the case. Not until Janet had researched the land deed did it become clear that someone else had water rights to *both* springs.

Looked for Water

Janet was still optimistic about finding a third spring. She combed the land, again shovel in hand, digging in any location that had a trickle of water. One site looked particularly promising. As she dug in the path of the seeping water, more water appeared. Gradually she worked her way up the trickle to a mammoth pile of dirt she had had bulldozed as she thinned the land of fallen timber and stumps. Under the pile was the third spring.

Although she was lucky enough to "strike" water three times, she emphasizes the necessity of carefully researching the land deeds. Are there easements? Rights of way? Water rights? Utility rights?

House Design

The classes then focused on house design. "The first time I built," says Janet, "I didn't realize how important it was to think out the relationships between different living spaces. You not only want to know what an area of the house will look like and how it will feel, but how it will function with other parts of the house and how it will be maintained. Before I had thought in terms of the parts—usually the wall or room I was building at the time. I'm afraid I still build more like a painter than a car-

The northeast corner, beyond the woodpile.

penter, but if a house is to function well, all the parts must work together." This meant giving careful thought to each activity and deciding which needs could best be met in which parts of the house. The design layout also had to include such practical considerations as light, ventilation, climate, and traffic patterns.

Fitting the Pieces

For months Janet went to sleep musing on the floor layout. "If I put the kitchen in the northwest corner, I have to put the bathroom next to it because of the plumbing, and the wood cookstove has to be there for easy access to the kitchen, which means the chimney has to go here. . . ."

Heating with wood caused its own floor plan confusions. Where will the stove be placed?

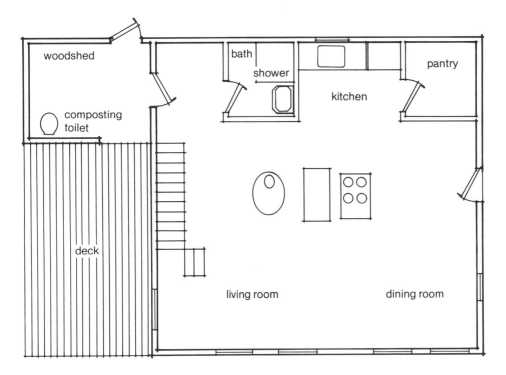

First floor.

Will there be enough room for people to sit around the fire and not obstruct traffic? Will the rising air from the stoves be sufficient to heat the upstairs or will the second floor be stifling? Will the woodpile be easily accessible from the woodshed yet also accessible in the summer to the outdoors? The process of fitting the pieces together seemed endless.

On her first set of house plans Janet had the stairwell in the center of the house. "I told myself it would provide a natural room divider, but I came to realize that there would be little headroom at the top of the stairs. In addition, I would be sacrificing valuable space in the center of the second floor. When I *finally* admitted that reality, I chose an L-shaped staircase running up the west wall.

"I was so used to the traditional Vermont farmhouse—dining room on the left, living room on the right, staircase in the center—that it was hard to get that design out of my head. Tradition is an overpowering force."

Question Everything

Janet says that one of the invaluable functions of her owner-builder course was to at least discuss, if not challenge, conventional construction techniques. "If you've only been in houses with basements, it's logical to assume that houses need foundations, but owner-builder schools make you question even such assumed fundamentals. You must be able to answer the question, 'Why do I want a foundation?' Otherwise you are paying money for expensive concrete walls you won't be using." The course made the students define their personal needs before translating them into a floor plan; the scrapbook was a graphic way to document this process.

From her personal experience in an owner-builder class Janet concludes, "The people who got the most out of the course and those who worked the hardest had already bought land and were ready to take the next step of building. Even those who were looking for land had a much better idea of what they wanted. Those for whom buying land and building a house were still off in the future had nothing

24

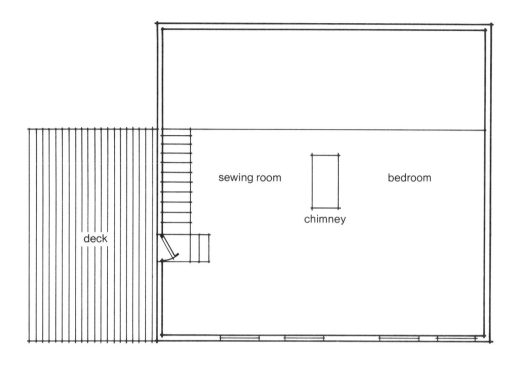

Second floor.

The Foundation

Janet's house rests on nine concrete piers. These piers are columns or legs sunk into the ground and upon which the floor joists rest. The holes can be dug with a tractor equipped with an auger attachment; by a gas-powered, hand-held, post-hole digger (which can be rented); or by hand. Janet chose the latter. She laughs when she talks of the concrete supports; the 24×26 structure is supported by only $100 of materials—and two months (on weekends) of back-breaking burrowing in the earth.

concrete to work with. Site does make a difference; it both limits and offers possibilities which may spark the imagination."

The holes were dug four feet deep (below the frost line, which will prevent heaving due to frost action), then belled out for the footings. This increases the bearing area of the vertical members and thus distributes the weight of the structure to more ground. The diameter of the piers is determined by calculating the dead load (the weight of the structure the piers will be supporting) and the live load (snow, wind, furniture, and occupants); the depth of the holes will vary with the local climate, foundation materials, soil conditions, and the load. Local building codes usually list proper sizes and depths for a given locale.

On the north wall Janet hit structurally sound bedrock within three feet, but the south

wall wasn't as simple. Headfirst down in the hole, she struggled her way through the last foot of each hole with a Boy Scout collapsible shovel and a coffee can. To get as strong a base as possible for the concrete, she had to fan out and level the bottoms of the holes.

Into each hole she poured six to ten inches of concrete which she mixed in a wheelbarrow. Once this footing had set, she slipped in the Sonotube. (Sonotube is the trade name for a cardboard cylinder used as a form when piers are cast in place. Sonotubes are available in different lengths and diameters.) Next, each Sonotube was plumbed, leveled with its neighbors, and filled with concrete. When the tube was full, an

L-shaped bolt (called an anchor bolt) was installed and temporarily supported until the concrete hardened. The bolt is used to hold the sill firmly to the columns.

Advantages of Piers

Sonotube concrete pier construction has much to attract the owner-builder. Unlike excavated cellars, concrete piers:

1. Substantially reduce the cost. Of the possible foundations, piers use the fewest materials; expensive grading and trenching are avoided. Storm tiles and gravel fill for drainage as well as backfill are eliminated.

2. Require little excavation. Only the holes must be dug, and these the owner-builder can do.

3. Demand less maintenance and less skilled labor in construction.

4. Can be adapted to almost any topography, allowing more freedom in site location. They are well suited to steep slopes and areas where you don't want to disturb what is under the house. They also can be constructed rapidly in almost any weather.

5. Leave the land intact. If holes are hand dug, there is little likelihood of damaging tree roots.

6. Avoid the necessity of having to install the plumbing early in construction.

7. Remove the annoyance (or worry) of leaky basements.

Disadvantages

The disadvantage of pier construction is that it leaves a crawl space under the house which is subjected to both winter cold and soil wetness.

To prevent rot in the floor joists, the ground below the crawl space should be covered with polyethylene plastic. The plastic will act as a vapor barrier and prevent moisture from rising out of the soil. To decrease the coldness of the floor above, it is necessary to insulate between the floor joists with at least six inches of fiberglass.

Plans for Space

Presently Janet has also stapled plastic skirting around the crawl space to prevent wind and snow from getting under the house. Eventually this will be removed; part of the crawl space will become a root cellar, the southern part will be incorporated into a 1½-story greenhouse.

Like other basic decisions (heat, water, plumbing, and house layout), Janet chose this type of cellar by deciding what she wanted and why—she had no need for a traditional excavated cellar.

Construction

Framing

Once all nine concrete piles had been cast in place, Janet was ready to begin framing. She says now that she could have worked up the lumber order herself. "All I had to do was know the spacing, then look up maximum span figures to decide whether to use 2×10s or 2×12s. At the time I wanted to be sure I wasn't about

"The (building) course made me think the whole thing through, from the dream to the interior detail."
Janet Macleod

Broad expanses of windows face the south.

to make mistakes I would be rectifying the rest of my life."

She bartered art work for having her teacher in the owner-builder workshop calculate the order of dimension lumber. These figures she sent to her brother, a sawyer in New Hampshire, who rough-cut the boards and seasoned them for three months.

Central Flue

The central flue was the next concern. It was crucial because it would vent the heating system—a Vigilant wood stove and a Canadian, four-lid wood cookstove. Since she had never worked with masonry blocks, she hired a neighbor-mason to show her how to lay up block, set the tiles, and cut holes for the smokepipe. Thereafter she finished the chimney herself.

In the meantime her deadline of December 1 was fast approaching and the roof rafters weren't yet in place. To speed the work she hired a carpenter for one month, but she says that if there had been time she would have completed the job herself.

About hiring help she says, "I'm slower and it takes me more time, but I've now done enough carpentry to realize that eventually I can figure out most problems. If someone knows more or I think they know more or if they think they know more, it's easy to take a back seat. But you always have an uncomfortable feeling. If you have only yourself to rely on, you gain confidence.

Wiring

Although Janet made schematic diagrams for the wiring, she had the house wired by a professional electrician. (Some of the drawings to alert the electrician are still on the walls.) Now that she has electricity, Janet has begun to question her reliance even on that source of energy. "It does seem somewhat ridiculous; I spent $1,500 for the panel box and the wiring. Subtracting out the monthly charge, I probably use only $.50 of electricity a month." Janet is continually reassessing her reliance on various household systems.

Plumbing

Janet is in the process of connecting the plumbing, which for a house on piers is always more complicated. Supply lines can't be exposed to freezing temperatures; post construction means there are always exposed pipes in the crawl space, and these will need protection until they get into the warmth of the house.

Usually a heat chamber or hotbox is built. It is a small insulated basement of treated wood or concrete block extending below the frost line with rigid foam insulation on the outside and fiberglass or rigid foam on the inside.

Sewer lines and water pipes pass into the earth through the hotbox, which is heated by one or two light bulbs located near the bottom of the box. A heating element with a thermostat can be used.

The Biological Toilet

Being involved in thinking through a total house design has led Janet to make other untraditional choices.

"In my first house I had water, a bathroom, and a septic system," she explains. "I guess I felt pressured, first by myself, then by friends. It was easier to go along with custom and put in a septic system. As I thought it over before building this house, I wasn't sure so much plumbing was compatible with the simplicity of my house, environment, or lifestyle. Then as part of my job I went to a conference on energy-efficient furnaces. The experts explained how furnaces could be made more efficient by installing heat reclaimers, more efficient jets, and clock thermostats, but these additional devices only mean that we are building more and more complex furnaces to do the simply job of providing heat. A wood stove does it all—and simply." (Janet burned only one cord of hardwood last year.)

She carries the reasoning further. "Why then shouldn't the septic system be as simple as possible? Aren't I giving up control of how I live if I'm always calling in someone else to take care of my things—and that's what happens when we design systems which we can't maintain ourselves."

Composting Privy

Janet has designed, and so far partially built, a modern privy. Privies are inexpensive, do-it-yourself projects. If the site is well chosen, there is no soil or surface water pollution; odors are negligible; and if the pits are properly covered, flies will be no problem.

The privy is next to the woodshed—with a southern view. It started out as a one-holer with two pits of concrete block construction. Both tanks are well ventilated and have clean-out doors to provide access for turning the excrement to aerate the waste. This aids in the decomposition process. Janet soon realized that because of the pit size, it would be some time before even one pit was filled. She therefore decided the second pit wasn't necessary.

Some heat is generated by the pile as the microorganisms that are responsible for the continuation of the composting process grow. However, the pile needs higher temperatures to kill harmful pathogens and parasites. Therefore Janet has decided to glaze the south-facing outhouse wall. The first bin will be filled with small rocks in hopes that the sun will heat the rocks, and this will in turn increase the temperature of the adjoining compost pit.

Grey Water

The composting toilet has reduced Janet's water consumption by one-third. There is only the grey water (waste from the sink and the shower) to dispose of. Her waste lines go into a drywell leach field. This is simply an excavated pit three or four feet wide and six or seven feet deep. Some drywells have reinforced walls or are backfilled with rock walls, then covered. Waste water percolates out of the pit through the bottom and side walls. Such pits must be constructed in permeable soils, with at least four feet between the bottom of the pit and the water table to prevent ground water contamination. Such a drywell system replaces the leach lines of perforated pipe, and is best used where percolation is good.

House Interior

The inside of the house is spacious and comfortable—and warm. Sunlight pours in through four large, south-facing Thermopane windows which partially light and heat the first floor. Janet thought she would need two stoves for heat; so far she's gotten by with just the Vigilant (using the cook top for simple meals) and the sun.

Janet has added her own special touches. The kitchen has a set of leaded windows which she brought from her first house. In a local salvage store she found a larger leaded window of the same diamond-shaped pattern. "It's ironic," she says, "the larger window cost as much as the entire foundation." But it adds a very personalized fillip to the space.

Two Skylights

The north wall has two skylights, one in the bathroom and one over the kitchen, for which she has taken a lot of ribbing from her "energy-minded" friends. "Originally," she says, "the skylights were for a studio space. When there wasn't room enough, I decided to keep the skylights anyway. I like having the natural light." There is also a special sitting nook in one corner of the first floor. It has pillows, its own window, and books on either side.

Skylight brightens the kitchen.

Under the stairs, a private nook for working.

29

Will Install Registers

Adjoining the house on the west wall is the woodshed, composting toilet, and the beginnings of a screened-in porch, above which a deck is planned. The upstairs has plenty of southern light and is heated by the natural convection currents of the wood stove. Heat registers are planned for the south side of the second floor to set up a natural draft pattern between the two floors. This system may have to be augmented by fans.

The Future

Janet's work is by no means over as evidenced by the table saw in the living room, a sink resting in the hallway, and the partially lathed walls. The walls are probably the next project.

Lath horizontally spans the open spaces between the structural framing with a ½-¾-inch gap between the wooden strips. The lath provides a surface to which the plaster can adhere; it has no structural function.

A base coat of plaster, containing a binder (gypsum, lime, or Portland cement); filler (sand, vermiculite, or perlite); and water is applied ½-⅝-inch thick to the lath with a trowel. A second coat is spread with a sponge float or stipple brush, if a textured surface is desired.

Old Method

For many years this technique was the prevalent method for finishing interior walls. Wooden lath has now been replaced by sheet materials or diamond-

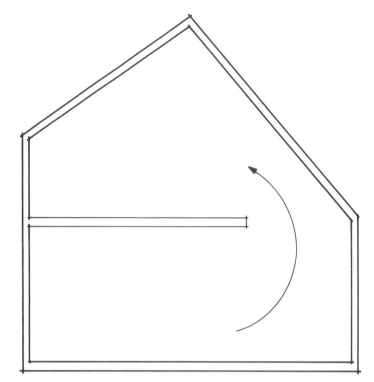

Air circulation to second floor.

Lath soon will be covered with plaster.

30

mesh, metal lath; by far the most common material for interior walls is gypsum wallboard.

Janet has rejected these in favor of plaster and lath—another labor-intensive project. She's already gotten a first coat of plaster on the kitchen walls and most of the lath has been nailed in place, but there's plenty left to plaster. The size of this undertaking doesn't seem to upset her at all. "I really don't mind living in unfinished space, because I enjoy watching the house gradually come alive around me."

Expensive Method

Unfortunately plaster and lath walls are proving to be more expensive than Janet had thought. "Lath," she explains, "has gone the way of all antiques. When a plane is sold for trimming doors, it has one (reasonable) value, but when it is sold to be placed on the mantle as a showpiece, its price skyrockets. So too with lath. They were flabbergasted in the lumberyard when I said I would start with twenty bundles (one bundle covers four square feet). About the only use for lath these days is for nailing up tarpaper skirting around a foundation. What is a common and usually cheap type of construction in one era becomes a lost art and hence expensive in the next."

Reasons for Doing It

However, Janet has based her choice on aesthetics, or maybe the delight she has in doing

Light pours through windows on second floor.

EXPENSE SHEET FOR JANET MACLEOD'S HOUSE	
Foundation	$ 115
Electricity	1,358
Lumber	3,859
Chimney	400
Roof	450
Insulation	1,000
Windows & doors	1,500
Nails	100
Miscellaneous	50
Interior	650
(Walls $400)	
(Trim 50)	
(Cabinet lumber 200)	
	$ 9,482
Labor	1,300
	$10,782

things with her hands, or maybe it is her interest in sculpting her own space. "I can't get the smooth surface with wallboard that I can with plaster," she says. "It may take a little longer, but it's worth it."

When the interior is finished it will be, like so many other things in her house, an expression of the artist, not the carpenter in her.

ABOUT THOSE HOME-BUILDING SCHOOLS

You'd like to go to one of those home-building schools?

But you hesitate? Maybe, you say to yourself, I'm too old, or not old enough, too inexperienced, a man, a woman, not strong enough, not bright enough, not handy enough with tools, or just not quite ready.

None of these is a good excuse.

If you have the interest, you'll be amazed how much you'll learn. And you'll fit right into the group. Why? Because the one thing all of the pupils have in common is an interest in housing, specifically building a house.

After that, the group is a mixed bag—men and women, young and old, handy and unhandy, well-educated and basic dropouts. All learning and working together, usually with a remarkable display of heartwarming cooperation.

The schools point out two things. There is a large group of us who would get deep, solid satisfaction from building our own homes. Too, there's an equally large group determined to own homes, and if building them is the route to take to make it economically possible, let's learn how.

Courses vary in length from brief ones, such as a single weekend, to cover specific aspects of house construction, to three or more weeks for complete instruction in building a home.

Costs depend on the school and the length of the course. Three weeks for about $400—not including room and board—might be average.

Students learn basics—how to plan, estimate costs, use tools—rather than spending time to learn how to build a specific house. That means the information gained can be used to build their houses.

Schools commonly schedule classroom work in the mornings, then have workshops in the afternoon, or guide students to houses under construction, for hands-on experience.

The students who get the most from the courses are those who plan to build as soon as school is out, who have a lot and a house plan, but who aren't afraid to change that plan as they learn in the school. Many students, for example, are exposed to the warmth of passive solar heat, or the cost-effectiveness of superinsulation, and revise their plans to include either or both in their houses.

The group is convinced, and for good reason, that if they do most of their own work (and some building codes will hamper this) and all of their own contracting, that they can cut 50 percent or more from their costs. Graduates with the time to go this route have done this well.

At the bottom of the class usually are those with only vague hopes for building. They lack the immediacy of a problem—how to get that house built—driving them to learn.

Here are some of the schools:

BoMar Owner Builder Center
Robert Bacon Jr.
704 Gimhoul Road
Chapel Hill, NC 27514

The core program, House Building Class, provides forty-five hours of instruction. House Building classes run three hours per session, and cost $300 per person, $450 per couple. There is a $25 discount for registration and full payment five days prior to start of class. The first class is free. Individual consultation costs $30 per hour or by contract. Seminars-workshops are limited to five to ten people depending on the subject being covered. Cost is $40 to $70 per session.

Colorado
Owner-Builder Center
1636 Pearl St.
Boulder, CO 80302

The housebuilding class is a detailed, lecture/slide/demonstration format course which covers all the processes involved in building a house. The seminars are designed to cover in more detail subjects that are important, but only touched on in the housebuilding class. Their hands-on workshops offer an opportunity to actually learn building techniques and use tools in a well-supervised jobsite situation.

Cornerstones School
Cornerstones Energy Group, Inc.
54 Cumberland Street
Brunswick, ME 04011
207-729-5103

Course offerings include: Energy Efficient Housebuilding, Housebuilding for Women, Energy Efficient Renovation and Solar Retrofit, Energy Auditor Training, Passive Solar Design for Professionals, Finish Carpentry and Cabinetry for Women, Timber Framing, Architectural Design, the Handywoman, Passive Solar Greenhouse Design and Construction. Class enrollment is limited. Courses are offered throughout the year. Fees vary. Room and board are not provided, but area housing is available. Evening courses are offered in the winter.

Fine Homes Unlimited
1461 Glenneyre Suite E
Laguna Beach, CA 92651
714-494-9341

Fine Homes Unlimited is a private design/building service that offers opportunities and resources that allow the lay person, owner-builder or owner-contractor to confidently and competently undertake a self-directed building project, as well as a consulting service that can assist owner-builders or owner-contractors with any phase of their building project, from design to completion of construction.

Heartwood
Owner-Builder School
Johnson Road
Washington, MA 01235
413-623-6677

Five three-week residential sessions in the design and construction of energy-efficient houses, from June through September. Tuition $475 per person, $850 per couple. Room and board from $300 to $400 per person depending on accommodations. Classes are limited to thirty students. Additional evening lectures include various self-sufficiency skills.

Minnesota Trailbound School
Of Log Building
Ron Brodigan, director
3544½ Grand Ave.
Minneapolis, MN 55408

Year-round residential session in log home construction, in Superior National Forest, Ely, MN. Tuition: $300/person, $500/couple. Course is entirely on-site, including all aspects of log building from felling trees to notching and fitting splitting shingles. Two five-day residential stone fireplace building course, offered in June and Sept. Tuition: $150. All classes are limited to fifteen to twenty students.

Northwest Owner-Builder Center
Tom Phillips, director
2121-1st. Ave.
Seattle, WA 98121

The center offers three basic series. Housebuilding (14 sessions, 42 hours, $250), Remodeling (15 sessions, 45 hours, $200), and Design (10 sessions, 20 hours, $175). Consulting services for special problems are $30 per hour. Courses are offered four times a year, and meet in the evenings and on weekends. Periodic workshops are available.

Owner-Builder Center
Blair Abee, director
1824 Fourth Street
Berkeley, CA 94710
415-848-5950

Several residential summer housebuilding courses offered in Grass Valley and Berkeley CA. Tuition: two weeks, $500 per person; three weeks, $600 per person. Room: $60 per week. Board: $70 per week (couple rates available). Several other classes in housebuilding and related topics are held year-round. They range from one day to forty-eight-hour classroom and on-site courses. Tuition ranges from $100 to $350. All classes are limited to twenty-five students.

Shelter Institute
38 Center Street
Bath, ME 04530
207-442-7938

Sixty hours of lecture and thirty hours of practical skills workshops offered in fifteen-week nighttime sessions, three-week compressed sessions, and two-week builder's courses. How to build a house, renovate an existing structure, or build greenhouses, barns, and underground houses. Lodging available. Tuition $375 per person and $600 per couple—builder's course and fifteen-week sessions $325 and $550.

Yestermorrow
John Connell, director
Box 76A
Warren, VT 05674
802-495-5545

Seven two-week residential courses will be offered from the end of May through August. These include four design-build courses, one course in basic remodeling and renovation, one Design course (for people who already know building), and one Building for Professionals course (for professional designers and architectural students). All courses emphasize quality design, building, and energy efficiency in owner-built houses. Tuition: $375. Room and board: $300.

BUY A KIT

A three-dimensional puzzle that you can solve, even if you're not a carpenter.

Thinking small as you dream of a home of your own?

How about a one-story, square, 144-square-foot house with a glass front, a shed roof, and a foundation of six husky concrete piers?

You and a friend can put Unit One up in four days—and never

By Roger Griffith

you mind that neither one of you can do more than spell carpenter, and both of you are confused by the little squiggles on a blueprint.

The cost: $3,500, as of 1982, and that includes a foolproof instruction book and all the tools you'll need for construction, even two stepladders and two carpenter's aprons.

Larger Models

If your tastes call for a bit more house than this humble beginning, Andy Prokosch will talk houses bigger than this. He'll discuss any sizes, up to two-level multi-bedroom homes practically of your own design. The kits his firm offers include several varied modules that can be fitted together into an endless variety of structures, with costs running up to $15,000 or more.

Andy Prokosch is president and founder of Shelter-Kit Incorporated, with headquarters in an old hydro power station on the shores of the noisy Winnipesaukee River, at 22 Mill St., Tilton, New Hampshire. He, his wife, Barbara, and their small child live in a sprawling, comfortable (Shelter-Kit, of course) house in the woods in Sanbornton, above Tilton.

Andy backed into the kit home business, starting in 1969. He, his three brothers, and their parents wanted a small get-away-from-it-all cabin on their eighty-acre New Hampshire woodlot.

His father, Walther, is an architect with impressive credentials for building everything from major airport buildings to the small cabins that fit so well into the environs of Little Dix Bay, the Rockefeller resort in the Virgin Islands. He designed the cabin, and all the family helped build it.

The cabin, the family declared, was a success. And it started a lot of discussion between father and son, about its potential, about how many other people there must be who want to build but are afraid to start, about how much pleasure and deep-down satisfaction they would get were they to build a cabin, then stand back and just admire it.

More than talk followed that construction project.

Andy quit his job at an electronics plant on the outskirts of Boston.

He and Barbara moved into a prototype of Unit One, in the woods.

And they created Shelter-Tech Incorporated.

Their first product was Unit One, offered in 1970. Their aim was to sell the kit to novice builders who wanted a small cabin in a remote area, far in the woods or on an island. The parts were packed in packages weighing less than 100 pounds each, so they could be backpacked or carried by canoe.

Unit One is still Andy's favorite, and it's the dream house of many who want an inexpensive yet comfortable cabin, as a place to get away from it all, in the woods, on the shore, or simply out back of the house; who want to build the cabin, but aren't prepared to build from scratch.

Can Be Expanded

He has added some components to Unit One, so that today the basic module can be expanded. These components include a 9×12 deck, a porch, or an enclosed porch which makes this a two-room cabin.

Some of the customers buy several units to put up as one cabin; others start with a Unit One plus deck, for example, then gradually add on other units. The illustrations show some of the possibilities, with the final one of eleven components covering 1,404 square feet. Further flexibility is offered by the ease with which the locations of windows and doors can be changed.

Andy saw an opportunity for a different type of building. He

From sheds and playhouses to log cabins (by the hundreds) and $100,000+ mansions, kits offer a broad choice for the would-be homemaker.

had run into a dislike of shed roofs that is common in New England, and had found, too, a desire for a two-story building. "No way will that shed roof hold a heavy snow," he was told. He didn't argue, although he knew the roofs would carry a load of fifty pounds per square foot. Instead he and his father went into more planning sessions.

Two-Story Model

The result was Lofthouse 16, a 16×16 building with space enough upstairs for a bedroom, bath, and storage area. It was first offered in 1978. Like Unit One, Lofthouse has a post and beam frame built of pre-cut, predrilled lumber and has screened sliding doors and windows, with insulated glass an option. Base price is $6,230. Modules that can be added include a deck, porch (just add a roof to the deck), or

Unit One: Work for four days for two persons.

lean-to (add walls), all 10×16, or a two-story 8×16 extension that can be attached to either the front or rear of the house.

Next, in 1980, was Lofthouse 20, similar to Lofthouse 16 but measuring 20×24.

Like Lofthouse 16, this one can be expanded by adding 8×20 extensions, or ten-foot lean-tos, porches, or decks of various lengths.

With the introduction of two Lofthouses, Shelter-Kit moved firmly into the construction of buildings for those who want year-round homes. Higher housing costs and interest rates, while discouraging many from buying conventional homes, stimulated interest in the kit house.

Week's Work

Andy estimates two inexperienced builders can put up Lofthouse 16 in a week. With heavier materials (but don't worry—the heaviest single element is less than 125 pounds) and a bigger house, Lofthouse 20 may take two weeks for two builders to construct.

These estimates of time are based on actual testing. Andy believes that the speed of construction is due in part to the quality

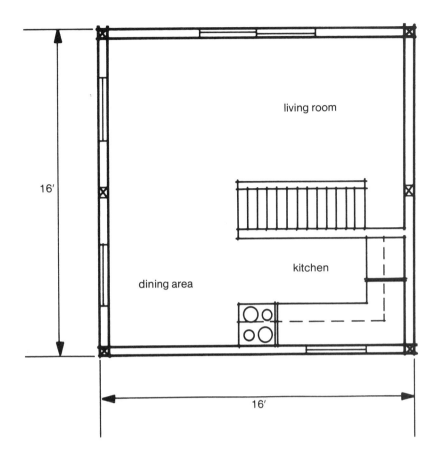

Lofthouse, a one-bedroom house with lots of storage space.

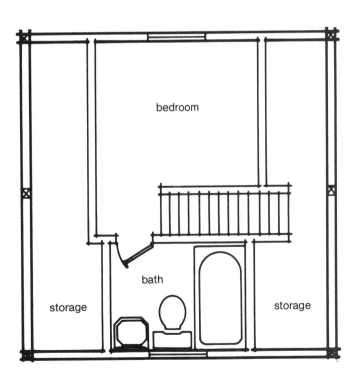

of the manuals he wrote, which spell out, step by step, the construction process.

He remembers having two inexperienced builders construct Unit One, to test both the kit and the illustrated manual. It was a lip-biting experience for him, but he kept still while the builders figured out the construction. They finished in less than two full days—and were proud of their work.

While the kits can—and are—shipped to many buyers, there's a trend for buyers to try to reduce this cost. They do this by borrowing or renting trucks and

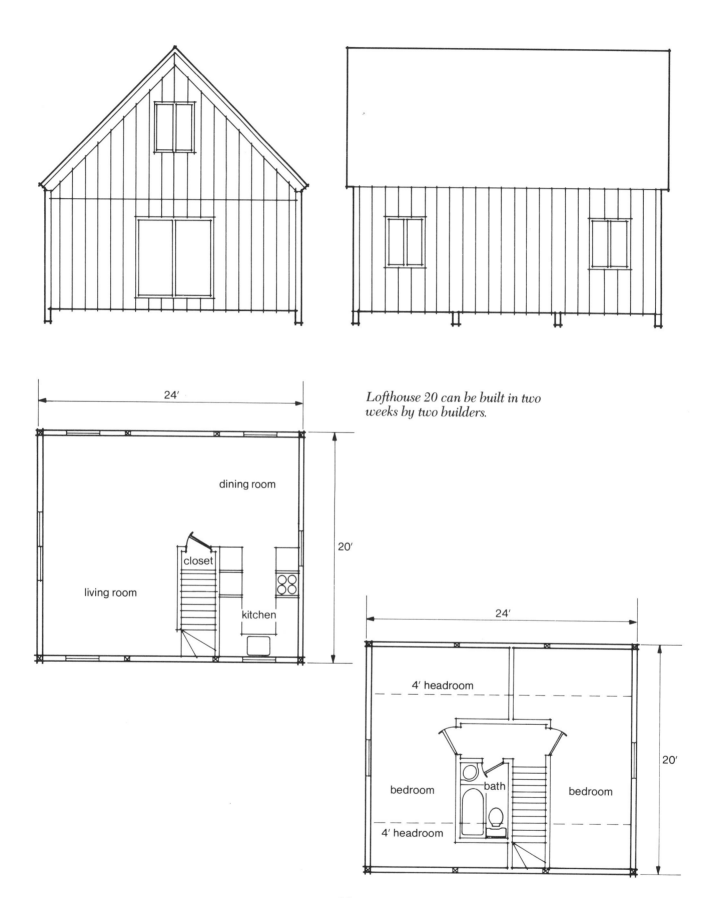

24'

dining room

20'

closet

living room

kitchen

Lofthouse 20 can be built in two weeks by two builders.

24'

4' headroom

bedroom   bath   bedroom

20'

4' headroom

38

driving to Tilton to pick up their kits. Andy and his force of four cooperate on such sales, helping on loading and the like. They emphasize that a pickup isn't big enough even for a Unit One. Weights range from two tons for the Unit One up to 13,000 pounds for Lofthouse 20.

Manual Sent First

When a Unit is purchased, the owner receives the manual first. That way, reasons Andy, he's more inclined to read the instructions before dipping into all of those inviting packages. Four weeks later, the kit arrives.

Andy says buyers worry most about the first step of construction of Unit One. That's to dig the six holes below the frost line, then, using cardboard forms, purchased from a building materials store, pour the concrete for the ten-inch foundation piers into these forms. The tops of the piers must be level with each other, the proper distance apart, and each must have a half-inch bolt threads up in the top. Andy stresses proper construction of the piers is "critical." (For those who like basements, the buildings can be placed on conventional foundations.)

If this is done right, little can go wrong in the construction. A saw is included in the Unit One tool kit, but there's but one small possible task for it—in case pre-cut flooring doesn't fit exactly in two spots. "Otherwise, if you have to saw, something's wrong," stresses Andy. He's familiar with most problems, and finds he answers questions that deal, not with the construction of

Bolts hold Unit One frame together.

the unit, but with such things as insulation, or how to provide water and a sewage system.

Success Stories

He knows of no one who has bought a unit, then failed to put it up, although some buyers have enlisted paid help to speed the job. The general reaction is just the opposite. Many have been so confident and enthused after putting up the shell that they have gone ahead with the re-mainder of the construction, such as wiring and installing insulation.

Buyers have used the kit houses, particularly Unit One, in a variety of ways. They've put them on foundations, complete with cellars, and used the cabins for year-round homes. They've carried them to remote interior sites in the bush, and many to the small islands that dot the Maine coast. Artists use them for studios; ski areas tote them to the tops of peaks.

Spacious Feeling

Enter a Unit One and, despite its only 144 square feet, there's a spaciousness to it. A big window (5×3) in the rear helps to create this feeling; even more responsible for it is the slope of the ceiling (from 7'10" in the rear to 9'2" in front) and the set of four-panel sliding glass doors topped by a Plexiglas clerestory.

For a small structure, the Unit One is stoutly built. Its frame is made up of 4×4 Douglas fir posts, 2×10 spruce floor joists set two feet or less on center, 2×10 spruce roof joists, and 2×4 studs. Siding is tongue and groove, 1×8 pine, with the same lumber used on the floor. Sheets of ¾-inch exterior plywood blanket the roof, covered with double coverage roll roofing, glued and nailed.

Andy and Barbara live in a Shelter-Kit house that's a model of what can be done by combining units.

It consists of four Unit Ones, three enclosed porches, and one porch and a deck. Rather than being cut up, crowded, and boxy, as these figures suggest, there's a pleasing spaciousness to the home, achieved through thoughtful blending of the units.

Use of the units, as this couple has done, offers prospective homeowners an opportunity to start small and inexpensively, and to create a larger home as money becomes available and needs grow.

Andy Prokosch home is a combination of nine units.

40

Deck dominates exterior of Prokosch home.

Why a Kit Home

From sheds and playhouses to log cabins (by the hundreds) and $100,000+ mansions, kits offer a broad choice for the would-be homeowner.

Their selling points:

1. You can save money (but not the 50 percent that some suggest).

2. You can see the house you select, before you build it, by visiting the displays of the manufacturers.

3. You can do much of the work yourself, even if you're not a skilled carpenter. The pieces are cut to fit, so construction is mostly a matter of fitting together and nailing together.

4. The kit offers real possibilities for a vacation home, a cabin in the woods, a starter home, and, best of all in some cases, a family construction project.

While your deal with a kit manufacturer will vary from company to company, you can expect, when you pay your money, to receive exactly what you contracted for—all of the pieces of the house, and all clearly identified, a detailed instruction book written in easy-to-understand English, sometimes on-site instruction for a day, and an opportunity to call the company for advice, if you run into problems.

House Shell

In most cases you'll be getting only the shell of the house, and you'll have to provide the heating, electrical, and plumbing equipment. Companies give a good estimate of this cost.

Many individuals have gained confidence in erecting a shell house, confidence enough so that, where it is legal to do so,

---

TOOLS AND SUPPLIES SUPPLIED WITH UNIT ONE

2 wrenches ¾″
1 saw
1 large screwdriver
1 #1 Philips head screwdriver
1 #2 Philips head screwdriver
2 stepladders 6′
2 carpenter's aprons
2 pairs work gloves
1 caulking gun
1 roofing brush
2 gal. clear wood preservative
3 tubes caulking compound
2 hammers
1 nail set
1 string level
1 carpenter's level
1 paint pail
1 paint brush
1 piece chalk
1 ball string
1 folding rule
1 linoleum knife
  hand cleaner

---

they have gone ahead with the remaining work.

Are there cases where the pieces of a kit home lie scattered on the ground, left there by a frustrated would-be builder?

Perhaps a few. But with the manufacturers, the builder, and the bank all working to avoid this, such cases must be rare. Manufacturers want a satisfied buyer, the best advertising they can get. Most buyers have worked out in advance how they're going to get the work done. And banks want least of all to end up with money invested in a partially completed home that seems destined to remain that way.

The success rate is very high.

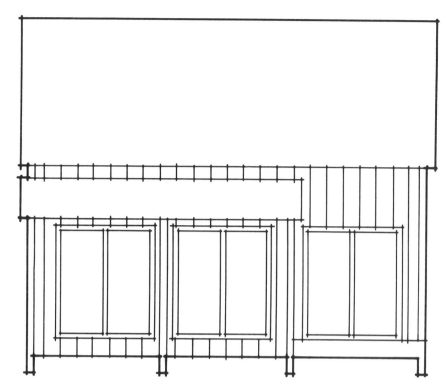

The Lofthouse and other models can be expanded in hundreds of ways. In this one, the Lofthouse was expanded with an extension, two lean-tos, and a deck.

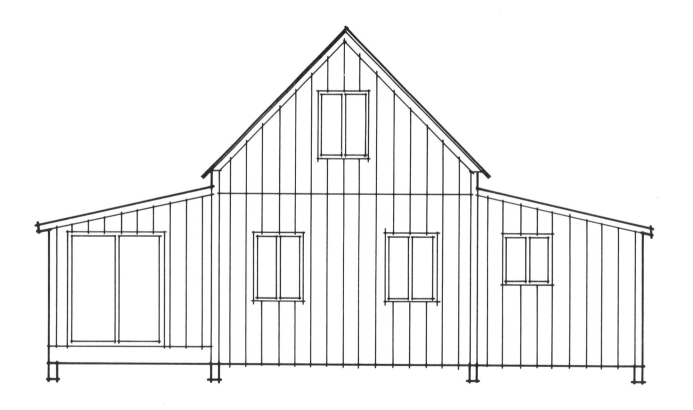

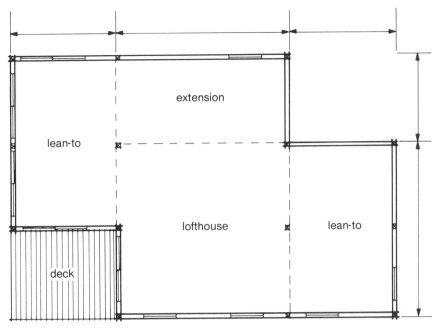

extension

lean-to

lofthouse   lean-to

deck

FINDING KIT HOMES

To find a kit manufacturer in your neighborhood that manufactures the type of house you want, see the *Guide to Manufactured Homes*, a 112-page book prepared by the Home Manufacturers Council of the National Association of Home Builders, 15th and M Sts. N.W., Washington, DC 20005 ($6.25, shipped first class).

This publication lists the names and addresses of more than 100 manufacturers of various types of houses. It provides a listing of which states each manufacturer serves, since shipping costs are high for long distances. It has twelve chapters, giving information about such things as determining the dependability of prospective builders.

Another approach is to visit building supply stores. Many of them carry kit homes. There's an advantage to working with such a store. It's handy in case of trouble. And it should provide you with a list of some who have bought and constructed such a house. Before visiting these, give the owner a break—and a phone call.

If you're considering kit log cabins, see the listings in *Build Your Own Log Cabin*, by Roger Hard, published by Garden Way Publishing ($9.95 plus $1 postage). This book offers much basic information on how to construct a cabin using a log cabin kit.

Kit manufacturers, for either log or conventional homes, sell their catalogs and descriptive materials. It tends to be of good quality, with fine pictures, and may cost as much as $10.

Changes Possible

A buyer need not feel locked into the plans of a kit manufacturer. Most companies will make changes, with the extra cost depending on the extent of those changes. Some manufacturers will even provide a kit from your blueprint.

As you arrange for purchase of a kit, you must prepare for delivery. These steps include:

1. Getting financing, building permits, and any other governmental approval required in your area. If you are in doubt about what you need, get information at your town or city offices. If still in doubt, hire a lawyer. This step might save you money in the end.

2. Constructing the foundation, after consulting with the manufacturer as to exactly what is needed, for the house and for the climate in your area. Of the many steps of house construction, this is the one most often left to the professional. Most errors of construction can be remedied with only the loss of some time and material; there's little you can do if you discover, midway in construction of a house, that the foundation is not square or not quite level along the top.

3. Preparing the site. The lot must have a road good enough for a heavy flat-bed truck to pull in on. You'll probably need this road earlier, when the foundation is built or poured. The flat-bed truck, of course, will be carrying your house, and you'll

SOLAR HOME PLANS

The Farmers Home Administration offers a plan (FmHA-2) that features an 1,100-square-foot, one-story, passive-solar home. The home design was developed by architects from the FHA office in North Carolina. The home is expected to achieve maximum solar effectiveness between the 30th and 40th latitudes (north of Jacksonville, Florida, and south of Philadelphia, Pennsylvania). The design calls for trombe walls on the south-facing side. The plan, presented on eight oversized pages, includes three floor arrangements to accommodate lots facing in different directions.

To obtain a copy of the plan, you must deposit a check for $5 at the nearest, local FHA office. Look in the Yellow Pages of your phone directory under U.S. Government, Department of Agriculture.

Other plans are available through the same office.

want it unloaded in exactly the right spot, so it won't have to be moved, heavy bundle by heavy bundle.

4. Planning shelter for the kit. You'll need a place for all the material—one that's weatherproof, and, in many areas, vandalproof. One that is sturdy enough to protect that material for several months.

Cheap Or . . .

Costs of kits and final homes vary from very low to over $100,000. Kits vary, too, in what you get, from a shell, without interior wall materials, to a house complete with kitchen cabinets. Few provide the bathroom fixtures or other plumbing, the heating system, or the electrical equipment and wiring. You'll find out, of course, as you explore details with a manufacturer before you buy.

Rules of Thumb

Here are two general rules about kit homes—and they're so general that they should be considered as the roughest of guides.

First, plan on spending double the cost of the kit for the completed house. Work out the arithmetic on this before you buy.

Second, you can save 20 to 25 percent, and maybe more, on construction costs, depending on your contribution in sweat equity. In some locations, the amount you can provide will be limited by building regulations making it mandatory to hire a licensed plumber or electrician.

Kit building offers a great opportunity for savings for the builder with lots of spare time (this is no weekend job), too little experience to tackle building a conventional home, and the humbleness to ask for or hire help when the going gets rough.

KIT CONSTRUCTION: A FAMILY AFFAIR

To save money, many kit-home buyers put together the many pieces that will be their home. And the work progresses much faster if there are friends or family members who can help. They need not be carpenters—availability, eagerness to help, and willingness to work long hours, those are the qualifications to look for when "hiring" free help.

A compromise method is to hire a carpenter, and then play the role of carpenter's helper (and pupil). The carpenter should be willing to work on a kit, and not out to prove that kit homes just don't work. Hiring help is especially useful to the novice, to get through the first steps, erecting the frame of the house.

Yet another method is for the buyer to act as contractor, arranging for subcontractors to build the foundation, erect the shell, and finish the inside, including the heating, lighting, and plumbing. (This method of home construction is explained in *Be Your Own Home Contractor*, by Carl Heldmann, published by Garden Way Publishing, $6.95 plus $1 postage.)

SCROUNGE

The savings you won't believe.

Linda Lindsey Photos

If you're trying to economize in building a house, it's a good idea to use standard sizes and common construction methods. That way you minimize waste because you don't have to cut things to fit. And you can often pick up materials on sale at lower prices.

But that doesn't mean that your house has to be "standard" or "common," says Michael Price, who has built a $2,500 house in Western Colorado.

A house shape that's becoming popular among people who prefer a cheap but unusual design is the polygon, Michael points out. No more square or rectangular houses for the younger generation. Four sides are out, and anything from five to twelve sides is in. The polygon can be built in various standard dimensions with post and beam construction using plywood sheathing for a minimum of cutting and fitting.

Michael and his wife, Tina, chose an octagonal shape for their tiny home nestled below the Grand Mesa in Delta County, Colorado. It was a matter of achieving the most space with the materials at hand for them. The young couple were working in a fruit packing shed three to six days a week just to support themselves, and their savings "nest egg" was sparrow size.

By Linda Lindsey

Basic shape of Price house is octagon.

They had begun to prepare for the task months earlier by accumulating lumber, largely through tearing down an old apple packing shed. It's the kind of work you can often find in this fruit-growing area, Michael says. He was offered the lumber free in exchange for removing the building. At the time he wasn't even certain that he would soon be building a house, but he figured that the wood would come in handy some day. If nothing else, he could resell it. As it turned out, the lumber was in-

Price house and, beyond, the Grand Mesa.

valuable. It was sturdy stuff—2×12s and 2×6s, with a few 1×8s from the siding thrown in. When the opportunity came to build, it was ready to use.

Commune Members

Mike and Tina met as members of separate but adjacent communes of young people. Between his junior and senior year in college Michael joined a "band of roving hippies" going to western Colorado in a bus. "I had worked my way through college," Mike says. "I mean worked—summers, nights, weekends, all the time. That was the first vacation I had ever had. It was wonderful." The school bus ended up on a beautiful spot of land just below the Grand Mesa, one of Colorado's scenic wonders (the largest flat-top mountain in the world, it is claimed). Tina was already living at a nearby commune started in 1973. The two took up residence in a tipi, then discovered that the land they were occupying didn't belong to either commune. They had to move.

While living in the tipi Tina and Mike became enamored of "living in the round." They considered building a dome because it would be quick and easy, but, after visiting in the domes of friends, they concluded that too much space would be wasted at the top. Another friend had built a two-story octagon with a staircase in the middle. This large a structure was beyond the means of the Prices, but the simplicity of the design appealed to them. They settled on a smaller-scale octagon with eight-foot sides. It would be a small house, but one that could be expanded from any section as the need arose. Just the thing for a new couple setting out. Mike and Tina were married in January and began pounding nails in the spring.

Luckily, they were able to acquire some land very inexpensively from one of the com-

46

munes. The county road cut off a small piece so that it couldn't be irrigated, so it was for sale. The Prices went ahead with their construction project even though the land transaction was not finalized due to the need for a survey. Just in case anything went wrong, they built so that the house could be moved to another site.

Dimensions

The dimensions of the lumber largely determined the dimensions of the house. With eight-foot 2×12 floor joists and rafters, the dwelling turned out to be twenty-two feet at the widest point between corners. First, poles were set up at each of the eight corners of the octagon. They were held in place by 2×8s clamped onto the poles by metal bands. The rafters were attached to a "king post" in the middle. After the rafters were all secured, the post was cut off, leaving the center floor space clear. The roof was then sheathed with 1×8s. A floor was constructed of 2×7s in an octagonal pattern—and what they called "Price's Pavilion" emerged.

In spite of Tina's misgivings, they moved into the pavilion just as the chill winds of fall began to blow. Since they had no glass, they covered the south-facing windows with plastic and discovered to their delight that they had a home they could live in. The bath as well as the kitchen were still outside for a while, though. Eventually a handsome, old wood stove was located to provide a source of space heat as well as for cooking.

It Worked

"It came as sort of a surprise that the house actually worked," says Tina. "We really didn't have much building experience. When we lived in a commune we learned about pole construction, but that's all. It's comforting to know that if you really want to, you can build your own house," she says.

According to Michael, the hardest part of the whole affair

"You have to be able to sniff out a bargain."
Michael Price

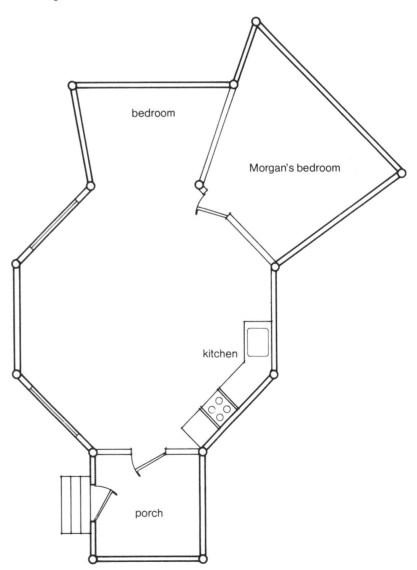

The Prices made additions to the basic octagon shape.

The Prices plan new house features.

the construction he encountered a neighbor who wanted an addition removed from his house. Even though the request came at an inconvenient time, Michael took on the job and thereby gained a lot of lumber for his roof and walls. "You can't be too picky if you've got no funds," he warns.

At first it was a one-room house. The furnishings consisted of a mattress and a chair. Before the snows came they managed to put up a plastic wind and moisture barrier and to insulate. Fiberglass was used in the walls because it was purchased at a good price at an auction. "I saw a big pile of insulation and when I looked at it carefully I noticed that the bottom layers were six inches thick, twice as thick as usual," Michael relates. "Some people thought I bid too high for the pile, but they didn't know about the thick stuff on the bottom. You have to be able to sniff out a bargain." Rock wool insulation made from refuse from Colorado steel mills was used for the ceiling.

Plywood Exterior

The exterior siding is plywood. The Prices bought the cheapest grade of exterior plywood since they expect to cover it some day with cedar shingles. That day hasn't come yet, but the plywood is wearing remarkably well, better than expected. The wide overhang of the roof has protected it somewhat from rain and sun, but weathering has brought out the grain in an attractive way.

In time, windows for the pas-

was getting started. You can sit around and agonize forever trying to arrive at the perfect design, he says, or wondering if you can actually do it. Once you begin pounding nails, though, and see the house going up, you get inspired. It makes you will-

ing to go out and work harder to be able to buy more materials.

Salvaging

Being willing to salvage materials is important if you have to build on a limited budget, Michael says. During the course of

All of these windows were salvaged.

sive solar array in the front were found in an old shed. Mike installed them so that they swing in and up to open, hooking to the ceiling. This way they admit plenty of fresh air without taking up space in the living room. Storm windows made of Plexiglas were added on the outside the next winter.

"Using old windows seemed like a good idea, but it turned out to be a big hassle," Tina laments. Finishing the windows was one of the least satisfying jobs she had in the whole building project. The windows had been painted and the old gray was peeling off—but not all of it. Tina tried sanding off the rest but ended up scratching the glass. A paint scraper was useless

too. In the end she just painted over the ragged edges and forced herself not to look too closely at the result.

What with all the salvaged lumber, windows, doors, and furniture, the Prices put out only about $2,500 in building the house. "We don't really know how much we've spent," Tina

EXPENSE SHEET

Estimates by the Prices of the costs of their house.

Land	$2,500
Well	1,500
Materials	2,500
Total	$6,500

says. "We should have kept records, I suppose, because now it's practically impossible to figure it out." She's certain of one thing, though: they can't have spent more on the house than they took in. That puts a ceiling on her estimate.

No Electricity Yet

Because of the cost, the Prices have thus far had to forego the luxury of electricity. All the work on the house was done with hand tools. "I'm almost embarrassed to admit that the entire house was built with two saws, a hammer, and a torpedo level," Michael says. "I should have gone out and bought a real level, but I was too tight." Last year he

49

borrowed a carpenter's level for verification and found that the structure is only a quarter of an inch off at the most. That's better than many commercially built condominiums these days.

Because the place is so far from the nearest electric line it would cost nearly $2,000 to bring in power through the rural electric association. Instead, Mike and Tina are exploring the possibility of putting up a small windmill. Their needs are minimal. At the moment they are using kerosene lanterns for light and a propane-powered refrigerator. Propane is expensive, but the refrigerator doesn't cost too much because it is used only in the summer. During the winter, foods are stored outside or on the porch during the day, brought inside at night. To avoid transporting food too often, the Prices rely on dried and canned foods

that Tina prepares at harvest time, as well as on whole grains that can be stored in tins.

Running Water

Water, they decided, was a necessity. "Sure, we have running water—I run out and get it at the pump," Tina says. It's an old joke and one that is starting to wear. Tina is anxious to get indoor plumbing, as soon as the weather warms up, she hopes. Her plans include a solar-heated shower. Drilling a well was one of the major expenditures they have made to this point. The bill came to $1,500 to go down eighty-three feet and install a casing and pump. "It's definitely worth the cost," says Tina. "Some people around here haul their water and store it in cisterns, but I just wouldn't feel safe that way."

The Prices have been able to construct a dwelling that is lacking the usual amenities because the county in which they live has no building code. This has been a major factor in keeping costs down and in allowing these do-it-yourselfers to proceed at their own pace. Of course, they would never have been permitted to build such a place in the city. Even the small towns nearby have building codes. But if you pick a spot in a poor county in the West, you may find that the county fathers have other problems that prevent them from worrying about how people build their houses. Delta County has a sanitarian who inspects septic systems, however, and when the Prices get around to installing one they will have to give him a call and pay their $25

fee in order to get approval. An electrical inspection is required before the power company will hook up a new system.

No Foundation

The absence of a building code made it possible to build without a foundation. Anticipating the need to move the house if the land deal fell through, and lacking the money to buy cement, Mike and Tina decided to sit their octagon on eight large rocks. Because the house is not heavy, they have gotten by so far with no problems. Some day soon, though, they plan to go back and dig a trench in order to pour a real foundation. Until they do so, Michael will feel uneasy.

Another reason for avoiding a concrete foundation was concern about disturbing the natural landscape. The octagon is surrounded by five acres, more or less, of sagebrush and juniper trees—a setting straight out of a western movie. So deeply did Tina and Mike care for the natural ecology that the couple actually carried in all their lumber and other materials by foot nearly 500 yards from the county road, crossing a draw with a little stream running through it. It wasn't until 1980 that they got a driveway, and that only because a neighbor happened to own a bulldozer.

Make Friends

"If you want to know how to build a house inexpensively," Michael says, "make friends with your neighbors." After having nearly completed the house without a driveway, the Prices made the acquaintance of a nearby bulldozer operator. One day he was off work and all of a sudden they had a path dozed up to their door. "At first we were disturbed about the destructiveness of it, scraping all the vegetation off the earth. Then we began to realize how nice it is to be able to drive up to the house with the groceries," Tina says.

Ells Added

As they gradually acquired funds and materials, the Prices added bedrooms extending out from the sections of the octagon. First came their own small room. "You could hardly call it a mas-ter bedroom," says Tina. "After all, it's only eight by eight feet." Then came a larger eight by twelve room for the baby, Morgan.

One lesson learned the hard way is this: "build before the baby comes." Although Morgan has been a wonderful joy for them, it is much harder to get anything accomplished with him around. Just carrying in the supplies became much harder. Where Tina used to have two hands to work with, one is now often required to hold Morgan's as he toddles along the path. He loves to get into the tools and make a mess, and stash things where you can never find them.

Mike conceived a way to re-duce the natural tendency to-ward entropy (disorder) in a small house: use built-ins. The only free-standing articles in the living room are a chair and the stove. The couches and table lin-ing the south walls are built in, as are the kitchen cabinets and bookshelves. That way nothing can get up and travel out into the middle of the room. It also makes it possible to tuck things under couches and other furniture. As a consequence, the Prices do not feel that they have a storage problem in their small abode.

Heating a Problem

Even though the house is small and well insulated, a means of heating it has not yet been per-fected. With no storage medium

Small ell in rear is master bedroom.

51

for retaining heat from the south-facing windows, the solar system works only during the day. The cook stove heats the house in the evenings, but it goes out at night, leaving the house icy by morning in winter. Their temporary solution is a little electric heater. Tina and Michael weren't bothered too much by the overnight fall in temperature, but they were worried about its effect on Morgan, who regularly kicked off his covers. The heater solved the problem, but it cost a fortune to run. "When we first got it we ran it too much. Now we put it on low and it keeps the chill off Morgan's room," says Tina. For a while they had an old coal stove but it proved unsatisfactory. Now they're keeping their eyes open for a sale on a wood stove that they can stoke so that it will burn all night and also heat water.

Front Porch

The addition of a front porch on the southwest corner of the building also helps to keep the house warmer. It forms an air-lock entrance, cutting down on the loss of warm air every time someone enters or leaves. And it provides a place to put coats and boots, as well as snow shovels, tools, and even toys.

Michael, an outgoing person who says his lifelong ambition has been to be a stand-up comic, is trying to help other fruit workers in the area to get ahead. He is employed as a job counselor by the Colorado Migrant Council, an organization that provides services to migrant workers and others involved in agriculture. He and Tina are setting an example of what can be done with determination and ingenuity on a small budget to get out of rental housing and on to independence.

BE YOUR OWN CONTRACTOR

You'll save money as you untangle red tape, arrange work.

Anne Wilson came from Craftsbury, Vermont; she has now returned, but not before living in other cities, towns, and villages, and in all kinds of housing: historic old farmhouses, apartments, tract housing, and condominiums. It has been a long way around, but she is now living on the piece of land she has always wanted, in the house she has been designing for years, and for which she did the contracting.

The day I stopped by, the temperature suddenly dropped to 9° F. Snow squalls restricted driving visibility to the dials on the dashboard. The roads were white meadows. It was Sunday; there was no traffic, even the plows were late.

In the distance I could see the board-and-batten saltbox, its windowless north side to the road. What a perfect day to test the efficiency of an energy-efficient house! It was windy. It was snowing. It was cold. It was winter.

Open Space

You quickly notice in Anne's house the sense of lightness and open space—two sets of sliding glass doors along the south wall, urethaned wide pine flooring, and white, white Sheetrocked walls. The space is sparsely furnished, making the visitor focus

By Mary Twitchell

on the subtle beauty of the staircase, centrally located in the living room. The treads are of ash, the risers of birch, and the fluted newel post, spindles, and hand rail are of maple.

As we sit by the wood stove, a mug of mulled cider in hand, Anne tells me, "I've always wanted to live here, ever since I was a little girl. My parents live just down the hill," she points to a red farmhouse, just barely visible in the distance below the ledge on which her house is situated. "My father is a farmer. Whenever we could get him out of the barn, which wasn't often, we would come up here on this piece of ledge for a cookout. It was always such a treat."

Gift from Father

She had asked him to "save this little spot for me." In 1974 he deeded her that ten-acre parcel. The land was unsuited for farming. It had ledge and was heavily forested with a mix of hardwoods (maple, ash, and birch) as well as softwoods.

Anne knew she would build her own home on this piece of land—someday. In the years of living other places in other structures, she had never found the perfect shelter. "It was either bungalow-, barn-, or ranch-style living, and that's pretty mundane," she says.

Then she tried (briefly) living in "a house of character"—the family farmhouse built in 1836. But that too had its problems. Everything needed repair. The walls weren't insulated; the windows leaked; the plumbing and wiring were twenty-four-hour preoccupations.

Anne continues, "There were financial considerations. I knew owning was cheaper, and I certainly prefer paying off a mortgage than paying rent to a landlord. I was also convinced that I could build without having to pay an architect, and probably do as good a job. Besides I wanted the gratification of designing my own space—something that was in keeping with the rural setting, the view, the climate, locally available materials, and it had to be energy-efficient."

The Perfect Time

Three years later Anne was again living and working in the vicinity of her ten-acre plot. Everybody was telling her this was the perfect time to build, but she didn't have enough money or quite the incentive. One day she spotted cardboard house models in a bank window done by students in an owner-builder workshop. She was fascinated; they were the kinds of living space she wanted. She soon

Board-and-batten saltbox in a Vermont hilltop setting.

enrolled in a fifteen-week course, going one night a week for 2½ hours.

Owner-Builder Course

"We were a real mixed bag," Anne explains. "There were fifteen of us, ranging from a real estate agent living in town in a traditional Dutch colonial (which he hated and his wife loved), to an 18-year-old free spirit who planned to spend the rest of his life living in a yurt. Some took the course as a hobby, some were Walter Mittys on the loose, some wanted energy-efficient ideas for future house renovations, and three of us already owned land and were eager to drive the first nail. Of those three, two of us have now built.

Most people got from the course what they wanted."

Classroom Work

Class was devoted to discussing site selection, different construction methods, the pros and cons of various designs (such as foundation walls vs. pier construction), house layout, energy-efficient ideas, personal desires, as well as considerations of solar, water, road, sewage—all those concerns that an owner-builder has before erecting a shelter. "We got very practical ideas rather than information on what weight hammer or what saw blade to use—those skills we would learn fast enough on-site."

Then each turned to designing a house. "We broke the house down into activities, then divided the house into various areas suited to each activity." Anne's previous experience with other living spaces meant she knew what worked best for herself and her son. "After living in so many cramped rooms," says Anne, "I knew I wanted one large open space with as little division as possible."

Anne was also familiar with energy considerations such as extra insulation and south-facing windows. "Heavens," she says, "for four years I had been planning. I knew what I wanted; I even knew where every receptacle and light switch would be. But I learned more from the course than I thought I would."

Won Confidence

Perhaps the most valuable function of the course for Anne

was that it confirmed her ideas and gave her the confidence she needed to tackle building on her own. As an important byproduct, it gave her procedural information and a complete set of plans.

To preclude turning back, Anne had the road bulldozed, fill brought in, and the driveway graded. Then she went to the banks with her plans to apply for Vermont Housing Finance money.

Financing

Anne had site plans, a foundation plan, plumbing and electrical schematic diagrams, floor plans, and house elevation drawings, but she knew that even as well prepared as she was, there might be problems.

"There were roadblocks every step of the way," Anne says, obviously annoyed that she had to become so well acquainted with the four-inch volume of FHA regulations. "They objected to the entrance (which is as small as possible with an airlock between the two doors). They said I had no 'front' entrance, and that what I was calling the 'front' entrance was actually a 'service' entrance. They told me I needed a concrete front stoop.

"They then disapproved of the lack of a 'traditional' two-foot by two-foot coat closet near the entrance. (I had chosen a much more practical, large, multi-purpose closet with bi-fold doors which is only five feet from the door.) In fact they went one step further by telling me that there just wasn't enough closet space in general. That I have a 28×30

foot cellar (840 square feet) and almost that again in the attic somehow didn't constitute storage space enough.

Lumber Regulations, Too

"The lumber was the next snag. I was going to take all the lumber from the land and use it rough cut. Housing Finance regulations require the lumber be kiln-dried, graded, stamped by an approved agency, and sawn two sides. This precludes anyone from using hand-milled or recycled lumber, hand-hewn beams, or hand-split shakes, without having them officially inspected. If someone had had to drive all the way out here and go through the lumber board by board, I wouldn't have saved anything by using my own trees."

"If you can balance a checkbook, read, and deal with people in a fair manner, you can build your own house."

Carl Heldmann
Be Your Own House Contractor

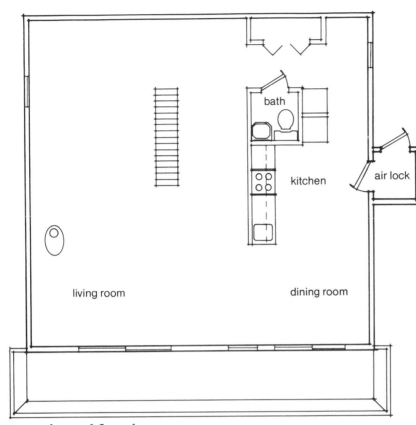

First and second floor plans.

Anne continues, "The list was endless. I was defying almost everything in their book of regulations. I also don't think being a single woman helped my credibility, and above all, I was going to be my own contractor. Part way through I listed Jim (the carpenter) as contractor, hoping that would help. But although he has had a lot of carpentry experience, the banks didn't know him.

"I assure you, I tried every bank in town, including the bank I had used for years. The answer was always 'no.' I was angry and frustrated."

A Little Luck

The rest of the story is a series of fluke occurrences—a bank director/friend of her father's dropped by the farmhouse while Anne was there, and within a week the loan had been arranged.

"I assure you, I tried every bank in town, including the bank I had used for years. The answer was always 'no.' I was angry and frustrated."
Anne Wilson

Anne advises any owner-builder to be persistent, determined, and patient.

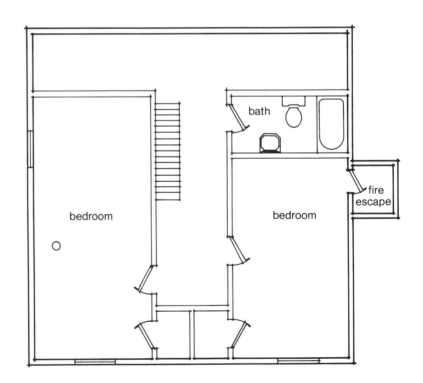

The hurdles weren't over yet. Anne's next problem was arranging the size of the loan. Loan officers base the amount they will lend on the basis of the cash-plus-assets of the homeowner-to-be. Then a bank appraiser places a market-value figure on the structure. Because the bank was so skeptical of Anne's cost estimate, they required her to take out a larger loan than she had asked for. "Well, I got a new refrigerator and stove out of the deal," laughs Anne, "but it certainly wasn't what I intended."

Code Complications

As Anne learned, code requirements, the bank, and the owner-builder are not an entirely compatible threesome. Code requirements exist to safeguard the health and safety of the customer from unscrupulous builders, but many of these regulations reach far beyond sensible protection. Some are even unnecessary (as owner-builders are well aware), and they can substantially increase the cost of construction. Among these requirements are: 2×4 walls sixteen inches on center, when twenty-four inches are adequate; double-framed 2×4s for window and door openings when single 2×4s are sufficient; or 2×4 interior walls when 2×2 walls are safe when they are non-loadbearing.

In addition, the code specifies all wiring be done by a licensed electrician; most owner-builders acquire wiring skills along the way.

Convenience, Too

Other requirements are decidedly providing conveniences way beyond health and safety requirements. Windows, for example, must comprise a required fraction of the floor area, ceilings must be seven feet six inches in the habitable area, heating systems (in some states) must reach 70° F. at a point three feet above the floor of all habitable rooms (which excludes wood heat because, officials say, it is impossible to gauge the Btu output of a stove). Hot and cold running water must be available (which excludes carrying your water from a well or spring, or preheating it on a wood stove, or using a sauna or bathhouse).

Code-approved sewage systems have received the most criticism. There are plenty of reasons to consider a composting toilet, especially on land with a high water table or clay soil. Nevertheless the code still requires that we dump our waste into water ("the five-gallon flush"), then into an expensive underground system, which may ultimately endanger our health, as well as that of the earth.

Owners Penalized

Although codes may vary from state to state, they generally penalize the owner-builder who is seeking an alternative or more simple lifestyle. The owner may, in fact, be much healthier and safer eliminating plumbing freeze-ups, hauling water from a nearby stream, and composting waste material. Certainly much less of this precious commodity—water—would be used.

Banks, of course, have had experience to merit their caution. They know that many owner-builders will probably express their disdain of "ticky-tacky" tract housing or cramped apart-

ments by building highly personalized structures. Many of these may be substandard and/or have very limited resale value.

Skills Unknown

It is also hard for a loan officer to evaluate the carpentry skills of owner-builders. Their skills tend to be questionable; in most cases this will be their first carpentry experience. Some banks have now made the proviso that unless the owner-builder is engaged in carpentry full time they will refuse to loan money on any do-it-yourself house project.

Owner-builders, too, have a penchant for leaving unfinished houses—or they build in stages. Banks want the house finished 120 days after construction begins; owner-builders average two to three years. At some point they usually run out of money or energy. The table saw still sits in the living room becoming increasingly part of the decor, and if no one has missed baseboards and window trim, there seems to be little reason to install them now. Those who build piecemeal take their time, gradually moving into larger and larger spaces

as another room or floor is completed. This way they have a chance to recoup from the physical, emotional, and financial losses of the previous building phase. Banks, however, make no allowance for these *modi operandi.*

Be Persistent

Anne advises any owner-builder to be persistent, determined, and patient. "At first the codes may seem impossible and the banks intractable, but eventually they may see you as a 'calculated' risk. And the owner-

Deck offers miles of viewing.

builder may have to make certain compromises (such as installing indoor plumbing or a conventional heating system). But don't give up."

Even seen from the banks' point of view, Anne wonders whether their experience justifies such rigidity. As she points out (and as is certainly true in her case), "the two-by lumber really is two inches wide (lumberyard lumber isn't), and I have a full six-inch exterior wall which makes for a stronger, more solid, more energy-efficient structure. I *know* that every stud cavity *is* filled with insulation. No one will tear off the Sheetrock and find there's no insulation. And the soffits have been insulated, the air spaces around the window framing have been plugged, and the windows were caulked—owner-builders build better, tighter, sturdier structures because they're building for themselves.

"I also know the lumber is better grade. Oddly enough, it has a lower moisture content than what is sold in lumberyards as 'kiln-dried.'" Air drying is simple enough for the owner-builder to do. The boards are stacked in a breezy spot on ground supports with stickers (spacers) every four feet between each layer of boards. Vertical flues are left in the pile so that air can circulate around the boards. Softwoods can air-dry in six to ten weeks of dry summer weather.

Green wood can be used on subflooring, sheathing, board-and-batten siding, and in all cases where the cracks will be

---

EXPENSE SHEET

Total costs of Anne's house were $34,000, or $21.25 a square foot for the 1100 square feet of the 28×30 house.

Reasons for the low cost:

• Lumber was cut from her lot. Total cost for sawing and delivering was $1,500.

• The lot was a gift from her father.

• She did her own contracting, and watched the pennies.

• Labor costs were $6 an hour.

• Careful up-front planning meant no expensive changes in mid-construction. As carpenters say, she measured twice and sawed once.

Some of her expenses included:

Driveway	$2,000
Water system	800
Wiring	2,400

---

hidden. On doors, window frames, finish flooring—wherever the boards are visible—the wood should be dried and planed.

Anne sums up the difficulties of securing financing by saying, "Unless you use a conventional plan, a well-known contractor, and traditional materials, you'll need heaps of fortitude and patience to get money from the banks. They're scared to risk on anything out of the norm."

She concludes, "Now, of course, the town is perfectly willing to assess my house at $14,000 more than I paid."

Contracting Yourself

Anne knew she didn't have the time to do the construction herself. She not only had to care for her thirteen-year-old son, but had a full-time job as evaluator of the state's 16 Voc-Ed centers for the Vermont Vocational-

Educational Advisory Council. However, she was going to be the contractor. Even though she had listed Jim as contractor, once the loan had gone through she immediately took over, as they had mutually agreed.

She began by walking the land with the sawyer (brother of the carpenter). They marked the trees, which were cut in May, sawn in June, air-dried and delivered when construction began in September.

Established Credit

In her role as contractor she then started buying supplies. "First I had to establish credit with the supply houses," she explains, "which meant providing three credit references. By buying all the supplies myself I saved the contractor's mark-up plus any discount I could finagle by buying in quantity and paying in cash. I bought everything—plywood, windows, doors, plumbing fixtures—everything except perhaps a pound or two of nails.''

Acting as your own contractor is a good method of reducing house costs. Usually a contractor subcontracts a lot of the work: the wiring, plumbing, foundation work, and grading. Subcontractors then charge the contractor who then charges the homeowner, adding his own mark-up to their work. This is standard practice, but also adds to the total cost.

Coordinator

Eliminating the go-between means the owner-builder is responsible for coordinating the job, dealing with the banks, the zoning board, and local inspectors, securing the materials, and hiring carpenters, electricians, and plumbers. It takes time, but if you are living in a familiar locale and have some idea of which firms to trust, the job will be much easier. Otherwise get estimates from more than one subcontractor. Compare these figures, then ask around town about their reputations before making a final decision.

If you're the contractor, you are responsible for juggling in their proper sequence all the things that need to happen. You must insure that the carpenters don't run out of materials or that the plumber doesn't arrive a day early, then is unavailable for weeks. The job demands a clear understanding of the order in which a house goes together.

Anne was lucky coming from a small town. She knew the people she was dealing with and she had

implicit faith in her head carpenter to handle the small decisions. She tells the story of visiting the site after work the day they began putting up the cellar walls. "I was horrified," she says. "That morning we had put in the corner stakes for the foundation, but when I dropped by, I knew the foundation had been moved eight inches to the east."

She ran to the phone; as she suspected, a rock outcropping had been discovered in excavating the cellar. It could be avoided by shifting the house slightly. "I knew so totally in my mind how the house would look," she says, "that I was able to catch such a small detail, and I knew from that day to trust Jim. Whenever he made changes there was a good reason. It's important to have faith in those you hire, especially if you can't be on the site all the time."

Amenities

Anne ran into no difficulty with water, sewage, or electric lines. There was an existing spring which only needed to be dug out. The soil could take a leach field and the wiring had to come 800 feet, which meant two poles, then the wires were run underground for the last 50 feet.

Energy Consciousness

"I decided to go with electric heat for back-up," says Anne. "Hardwick has the cheapest rates in the state, and since I'm away because of my job, I wanted to be able to set a thermostat and not worry." Most of

the time, however, the house is heated with the Vigilant wood stove, which burns three cords a year.

Anne has incorporated other energy-efficient ideas. The north wall has no windows. This unnerves her mother, who is convinced that all prowlers come from the north. Anne concedes that at night in her second-floor bedroom she periodically doesn't hear cars driving up (they approach the north side of the house), but that doesn't bother her.

The walls have six inches of insulation, now standard construction practice. There are twelve inches of fiberglass in the ceiling, and all windows are double-glazed.

Made Thermal Curtains

Anne has made her own thermal curtains—cheap and quick. "I bought the loudest sheets I could find at K-Mart. I sewed pleater tape to the tops, then adhered aluminized foil and batting with fabric cement to the window-side of the sheets."

The aluminized foil, sold as "Astrolon" or space blanket, is two layers of metallized polyethylene with a layer of tridirectional glass scrim between. It raises the R-value of windows to 5. (Each layer of window glass has an R-value of 1.) The Astrolon reflects heat in the house back into the rooms, much as a mirror would, and creates a dead air space between the glass and the room. This reduces heat loss through the cold glazing. The material is available in different colors (approximately

Living room sliding door leads to deck.

$1.75/yard) from Shelter Institute (38 Center Street, Bath, ME 04530).

To prevent drafts, Anne has stapled the edges of the sheets to the framing. "Insulated curtains," she says, "have made all the difference and though the Astrolon crinkles, the curtains only have to crinkle twice a day, once when they're opened, and again when they're closed at night."

Next Time

Anne admits to making a few mistakes, but nothing she can't live with. "I'd do it again in a minute," she says of home building, but she would change some things.

Next time she would do without a cellar. "I built one," she says, "because my friends said I needed one, though they couldn't tell me why. And I sort

of thought I needed one, but I didn't know why. Now that I have one, I still don't know why." She did reduce the conventional cellar height, floor-to-ceiling, to six feet, and the walls are earth-bermed to prevent the pipes from freezing.

Concrete block foundations such as Anne's are extremely common. They are good for insulating the upper floors, and for the extra basement space. They can be used in all types of soil because they distribute the load of the house over a large area, but the concrete blocks and poured footings do add appreciably to the expense.

Wood Storage

Anne uses the basement for storage—mainly for storing wood, which then must be lugged upstairs to fill the wood box. The cellar has both a door to the outside and a window for throwing in the wood, but an outdoor woodshed would have been cheaper and just as efficient. She had thought of moving the wood stove to the cellar, which would be trading the task of hauling the wood upstairs for having to go down cellar every time the stove needed to be stoked. Anne advises future

builders to seriously consider going with concrete piers unless there is a *real* need for cellar space.

She has also reconsidered the staircase. At first it was located along the west wall, then moved to the northwest wall, and finally to the center of the living room. Since she doesn't need the stairwell opening for the passage of heat (the stovepipe radiates so much heat to the second floor that her son often sleeps with the window open), it could be located elsewhere. When the room is crowded, however, it provides extra sitting space, and the workmanship certainly justifies its prominent position.

Size of Windows

Along the south wall Anne has one set of sliding glass doors for

the dining/kitchen area, another set in the living room, but she says, "I might have replaced the two-foot by two-foot window between them with floor-to-ceiling windows, making the south wall almost solid glass."

From the sofa along the interior wall it is hard when seated to get the full southern panorama. Anne emphasizes that window placement is vital, not only where you want the windows when you are standing but also when you are seated. But adding more glass does mean sacrificing wall space.

Anne also thinks she might like an expanded airlock at the front entrance. "As you can see, once you begin storing a rake, a snow shovel, and two pairs of skis, the entry is filled. Nor am I sure I want to jump into this mess in case of fire." Since the wood stove is on the west wall, it made sense to include a fire escape on the east wall. It's a trap door from Anne's bedroom which leads to a ladder in the entryway. A full-sized mud room would have taken care of that problem as well as providing more room for storage of miscellaneous outdoor equipment.

Pine Flooring

Another area about which she is still deliberating is the floor. She carpeted the second floor for warmth, but thinking carpet was more expensive than pine flooring, she chose the latter for the first floor. "Jim was adamant," she admits. "He wanted nothing to do with this floor, and he was right. I knew I'd be tracking dirt up from the cellar every time I

Dining room, as seen from kitchen.

Anne wishes this entrance was larger.

brought in a load of wood. I knew it would ruin any rug, so I insisted," she adds sheepishly.

The flooring has shrunk, as Jim forecast, leaving an ⅛-inch gap between the boards. Had the boards been stored indoors in a heated part of the house for six weeks, they would have done their shrinking before they were laid. At this point Anne may have to go with carpeting or lay a second floor. But even with the gaps, the wide pine flooring adds a beautiful, light, rustic touch.

As I left the warmth of the house, the storm abated. It was silent. To the south I could finally see Eligo Pond down below the ledge—the surrounding hills of evergreens protecting its beauty, and a board-and-batten house on the bluff keeping watch over the entire valley. Any tussles with the banks seemed a small price for waking to this view.

GO UNDERGROUND

Keep costs low, and save later, too, on fuel bills.

There was a homey smell in the air, an apple kind of smell.

An apple pie, or maybe apple cake or apple pastry, was baking in the oven.

Penny and Amber were barking and making a genuine scene because Bob and Mary Jane Frechette were receiving visitors, and country dogs are expected to bark on such occasions.

There was plenty of cut-up wood outside, because this is Maine and in Maine prudent country folk burn wood when it gets cold.

The only thing missing from this Currier and Ives rendering of life in the country was the rambling country house; in fact, if Currier and Ives were ever to trek out to the Bauneg Beg region of North Berwick, Maine, in search of such illustration, they'd be at a loss when they reached the Frechette household.

An Affordable Home

The Frechettes live in a house, of course, but not the kind of house you'd expect to see out in the country. Call them cave-dwelling pioneers if you want, but they have discovered that the truly affordable American home is not a two-story Cape in the suburbs but a one-story hide-

By Steve Buckley

away that's buried in the side of a hill.

Some call them "underground homes" and the artsy-folksy types might call them "earth-sheltered homes." Call them what you will, except expensive.

The Frechettes built what is basically an in-the-ground home in 1979 for only $38,000, far less than the average American Dream is going for these days. The house was built into the ground on a thirteen-acre spread, with only the front wall and roof visible, while the other three walls separated rooms from the earth.

In a word, the home is unusual, but, flirtations with the unorthodox aside, simple logic was applied when the decision was made to go under.

Plenty of Privacy

"Out here, we have plenty of privacy and this is a house that I can afford," says Bob, 42, a Sanford, Maine, firefighter who dabbles in real estate, chimney cleaning, and other enterprises.

"This is," he says, "the affordable American home. It's easy to heat, easy to operate...."

"And it's easy to maintain," adds Mary Jane.

The cave, then, is easy. It's also comfortable, modern, and expensive looking.

Not expensive. Just expensive looking.

For their $38,000 investment, they have a home that is sixty-six feet long and thirty feet wide, with eight-foot ceilings. Along with their living room, kitchen, two bedrooms, and a bathroom the size of the Yankee Stadium outfield, they also have a two-car garage that is twenty-four by thirty feet.

When they set out to build their dream house, the Frechettes decided that it would be their retirement home. They wanted, as Bob puts it, "a house that would last 100 years." By doing comparative shopping and buying only the best materials, they may have just such a home.

Estimate: $90,000

The Frechettes had done a considerable amount of reading on this new concept of living, and paid an engineer $500 to draw up blueprints. But the estimate for his plan was $90,000. "And we certainly couldn't afford $90,000," Mary Jane says.

The solution? Put the $500 blueprints on a shelf somewhere and go out and play engineer. So Mary Jane, who as a teen-ager was whisked away from her South Carolina home by a Maine Marine named Bob Frechette, went down to the library, did some research, and designed her own in-the-ground home that they could build for $38,000.

The Frechettes in front of their 'affordable' home.

Expenses

The major expense was $13,-000 for landscaping, and for concrete and steel work. This included the backfilling and shaping of the land to rid the foundation of excess water.

Eighteen inches of sand and gravel were applied to the undisturbed ground, with concrete footing penetrating the sand and gravel. Next came a plastic vapor barrier, four inches of concrete, and a coat of Thompson's water seal. Drain tiles are affixed to the footings.

They paid $7,000 for roof trusses, interior doors, mirrors, plywood, and 2×4s for studding.

Other expenses include $2,500 for kitchen appliances (stove, refrigerator, and dishwasher); $2,000 for wall-to-wall carpeting and installation; $1,600 for an artesian well, pump, and fixtures; $1,000 for commercial-grade steel exterior doors and Thermopane windows; $1,145 for lumber and building supplies; $500 for finishing Sheetrock; $500 for two double Thermopane skydomes; $500 for a cast iron woodburning stove; $500 for those blueprints; $400 for rigid foam insulation; $300 for waterproofing materials; $100 for soil tests; $100 for building and plumbing permits; and $50 for 500 used rubber tires that were used behind the walls.

Labor costs amounted to $6,394, with $2,394 being paid for electrical work, $2,500 for carpentry and $1,500 for plumbing.

Bought the Best

Mary Jane, as good an accountant as she is an in-the-ground house designer, has kept every bill and receipt and can break down the building costs almost to the penny. "There were a lot of things we could have cut out to reduce the costs," she says,

65

"but we wanted to get the best of everything. Remember, this is our retirement home."

"We figured that if we built the house this way," adds Bob, "there'd be a lot less things we'd have to fix or replace in the future. When we bought materials for this house, we never bought cheap materials. Everything here is the best you can get."

A young couple thinking of building an in-the-ground house, then, could actually build for less than the $38,000 price tag?

"Definitely," says Bob. "Other people wouldn't necessarily have to build with the same materials we did." He used the kitchen appliances as an example. They paid $2,500 on kitchen appliances, but, says Bob, "you could maybe spend $1,500. Or you might already have kitchen appliances when you built."

Similarly, the $2,000 spent on carpeting could be reduced or eliminated. "We could have installed a tile floor much cheaper, but the carpeting helps to insulate out the earth's temperature," Bob says. "We like that extra warmth. Besides, we like carpeting better anyway."

The roof of the house is covered with $2,000 worth of tar and gravel, but $800 worth of asphalt shingles would have sufficed. "The way the roof is now, we'll probably never have to bother with it again," Bob says. "I think we'd be replacing asphalt shingles in a few years."

There are many other ways to cut costs when building an in-the-ground home. The Frechettes' bathroom fixtures are super deluxe. You could perhaps

Patio area is sunny and protected.

do it cheaper. The front wall could have been built with 2×8 wooden beams, instead of the poured concrete that was used. And there's a thirty-foot firewall separating the living room from the two-car garage, which is at the left of the house. You could even get by without the garage.

Got Estimates

"Plus," says Mary Jane, "we could have done a lot of the work ourselves. We contracted a lot of work out to different places, but we always got estimates first. That's important."

It should be noted that by purchasing only the best materials they will derive long-term benefits because of the money they save in the future maintenance. The heavy insulation and carpeting also will save on heating costs.

The only heating cost the Frechettes had in their first winter in the house was the price of gasoline to run a chain saw. All they needed were two cords of wood for the stove, and they have plenty of wood on their land.

The double Thermopane skydomes in each bedroom provide passive solar heat and three of the house's walls are protected by earth, so the temperature never falls below 55° F.

Never Cold

"It could be ten below zero outside and you wouldn't know it if you stayed in the house," Bob says. "We haven't had a day yet when we've been cold in here."

The Frechettes do have two electric heaters, but they've never been used. "The bank made us get them," Bob says.

In the summer, Bob estimates the temperature was fifteen degrees lower on the average than during their previous summer in a conventional house. The humidity usually stayed at fifty. They have found that when the humidity drops to forty-five they are susceptible to electrical shocks when walking on the carpeting or when coming in contact with the two family dogs. They avoid this by opening the front windows to ventilate the house. This raises the inside humidity to the outside humidity,

and Penny and Amber no longer have to worry about starving for the masters' affections.

The only time the house ever gets warm during the summer is during this ventilation period, since the inside temperature will rise with the humidity. On days when it is extremely humid outside, the Frechettes have a dehumidifier on hand. "The only time we use that," explains Mary Jane, "is when it's very humid outside."

The walls of the house contrib-

ute to its coolness in the summer, just as they contribute to its warmth in the winter.

Insulated Wall

The front wall, the only wall in the house that does not face the earth, is constructed differently from the three other walls since it does not have to withstand much stress. Excluding the garage, it is forty-two feet long and is faced with clay bricks. One inch of foam insula-

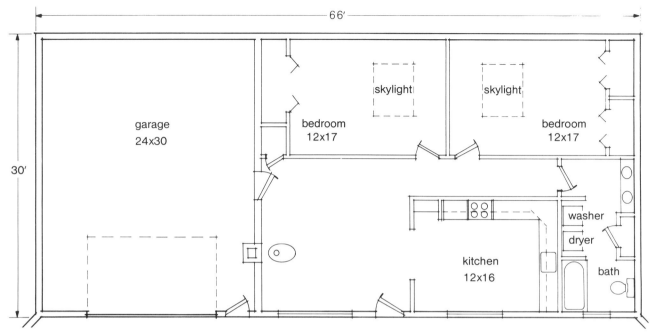

Skylight brightens this bedroom.

"The underground house movement had to overcome a host of anxieties, both real and unfounded. Living underground is a radical proposal, a more extreme departure from the American ranch than superinsulation, greenhouse-sunspaces, or double-envelope construction. But the earth-sheltered houses proved themselves early on, and the pioneers spread the word: the houses were dry, light, airy, and energy-efficient, warm in winter, cool in summer."

Don Metz
Superhouse

tion comes next, separating the clay brick from eight inches of poured concrete. A coat of water seal was put on the concrete, and twenty-four 2×4 studding beams are spaced vertically two feet apart along the front wall, covered with a half-inch of Sheetrock.

After the Sheetrock, you're inside the house. The Frechettes opted for white paint inside, and they let modern, colorful furniture do the talking.

Strong Walls

The back and two side walls were designed to withstand the stress from the earth. To keep all wood from touching the earth and contracting moisture, the Frechettes covered the walls with a plastic vapor barrier. The walls consist of three inches of rigid foam insulation, an eighth-inch of tar paper and foundation water sealer, plus a ten-inch

thick barrier of poured concrete. Like the front wall, 2×4 studding beams were used behind a half-inch of Sheetrock.

The side walls are both thirty feet in length.

A three-foot high barrier of used tires is at the base of these three inside walls to aid in drainage of water from the vapor barrier.

"We could have used gravel," says Mary Jane, "but the tires are cheaper and do the job."

Slanted Roof

All of which brings us to the slanted roof, which was constructed with as much thought and logic as the walls and floor. Including a front overhang, it measures thirty-four by sixty-six feet and is covered with tar and gravel over five-eighths of an inch of plywood.

The plywood base is supported by thirty-four 2×6 trusses

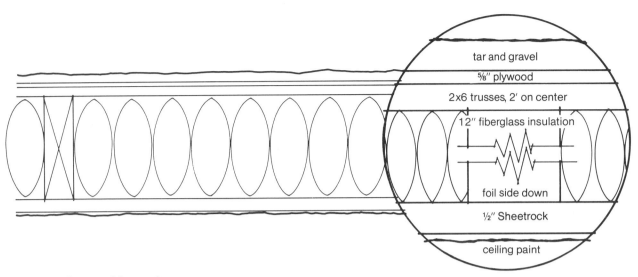

tar and gravel
⅝" plywood
2x6 trusses, 2' on center
12" fiberglass insulation
foil side down
½" Sheetrock
ceiling paint

The many layers of the roof.

spaced about two feet apart, and below that there are twelve inches of fiberglass insulation, foil side down, and a half-inch of Sheetrock.

Because of the strength of the four outside walls, none of the inside walls is a supporting wall, meaning that at the Frechettes' discretion any wall can be torn down to create a third bedroom out of the two large ones already in the house.

The only openings on the roof are the chimney and the sky-dome windows, one in each of the two bedrooms.

The skydomes are two by four feet, with an air space between two layers of Thermopane glass. They extend eight inches above the roof of the house, and can be opened and closed at the Frechettes' discretion.

When a house is buried in the earth as this one is, moisture would seem to be an obvious problem. But the precautions the Frechettes have taken seem to have worked; they haven't complained of any moisture problems yet, save for some condensation that builds on the inside of the skydomes in the morning. "And it doesn't drip or anything," Bob points out. "They fog up with condensation sometimes, but that's about all."

But that's not the only prob-

Foundation was designed to eliminate moisture and heat-loss problems.

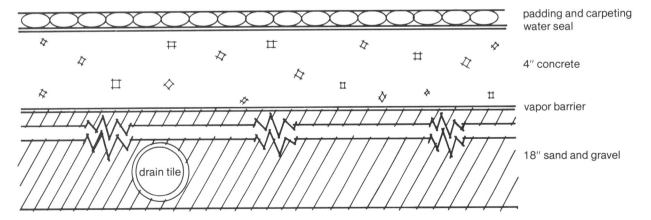

padding and carpeting
water seal
4" concrete
vapor barrier
18" sand and gravel
drain tile

lem they have had with their skydomes. It's not that they don't work—they work too well. "They let too much light in," Bob says. "Once the sun comes up in the morning and it starts coming in through the ceiling, it's almost impossible to sleep."

Since Bob is, after all, a firefighter with night duty sometimes, something will have to be done. They are planning to build shutters, which will either welcome the sun or block it out, depending on his sleeping habits at the time.

Possible Change

If they could start again, the only change they would make in the house is the bathroom. There is only one window in the room, on what is the front wall of the house, and they have wanted more natural light in the bathroom. They are planning to add a skydome window, similar to those found in the bedrooms, and they'd also like to put one in the garage. "The way the ceiling is constructed, it wouldn't be hard to do," Bob says. "In some houses, it's not as easy to add windows."

The bathroom closet houses a stone-lined hot water heater, along with a water pump and filter. The heater runs on electricity, but the Frechettes plan to install a solar heating panel to do the work. In any event, the heater now is in operation only four hours a day, and Mary Jane claims that there has never been a lack of hot water. "If we had children running around here, we'd most likely have it running all the time," she says, "but as it is now, it could go off and we still have plenty in the tank."

All water pipes run underground from a well to the house and are enclosed in an outer pipe that makes maintenance a cinch. Should the pipe require maintenance all that they have to do is dig at the well, and pull the entire pipe out through the outer pipe. This eliminates digging anywhere but at the well, preserving the landscaping as well as saving time and money.

Many Questions

They have been fielding questions about their house from the day they moved in. It's not every day that you meet a couple whose bedroom windows are on the ceiling, so, naturally, there are questions.

The most common misconception that they have to deal with

Broad windows on south side plus skylights make this a bright home inside.

is, as Bob puts it, "people thinking we live in some dark cave."

"There are people who think that we live in this dark, dreary hole filled with frogs and spiders," Mary Jane adds. "And I can assure you, there are no frogs or spiders here."

No, no spiders or frogs. But plenty of vegetation since they have an abundance of plants hanging throughout the house. The plants, plush carpeting, and white walls give the house a "clean" look, free from the loud walls that make other dwellings look cramped. A spacious, uncluttered hallway connects the living room with the two bedrooms and with the bathroom, which is at the end of the hall. The two-car garage can be en-

tered from the living room, as can the kitchen, which is at the right of this room.

Landscaping Ahead

While most of the decorating inside has long since been taken care of, there is still much to do outside. In fact, there are thirteen acres of work out there.

The toil began with landscaping in front of the house, and what was once a barren plain of dirt is slowly turning into a lawn. The dirt road that connects this in-the-ground hideaway with the rest of the world is scheduled to be paved, and they have both a $3,000 greenhouse attached to the house and an outside garden.

It's truly life in the country,

The only heating cost the Frechettes had in their first winter in the house was the price of gasoline to run a chain saw.

but it's also life on the farm. They built a barn about 100 feet to the left of the house, and new members of the family include twenty-six laying hens, two pigs, and a flock of geese. The barn cost $5,000.

Planning a Pool

They'd like to build a pool, too, but with all the money they've invested in other projects, this is one luxury that will probably be put off for another summer or two.

North Berwick's rural setting and five-acre zoning laws mean that the Frechettes need not fear being swamped by neighbors, but the novelty of their home means they're receiving guests constantly.

"If this house were in the city, there could be a problem of people coming by and walking on the roof," says Mary Jane, "but

out here, that's no problem. You can't even see the house from the road."

People manage to find it. One clue is Bob's sign that warns that his dogs, Penny and Amber, eat oilmen. That's his way of saying that he's found a better way. The Frechettes would rather let other people worry about the high cost of oil. As long as the chain saw has gasoline in it, fuel will not be a problem.

Big Savings

"This house saves us $2,000 a year in heat, power, taxes, and insurance," says Bob, "so you have to figure that it will pay for itself in twenty years."

No, it will pay for itself in less than twenty years, inflation being what it is. That means that their idea was a good one and a money-saving one. And they think others might like to "go

under." Because of all the publicity their house has received— and there have been plenty of telephone calls and visits from strangers—the Frechettes have turned their abode into a model home. They've gone so far as to have additional blueprints printed, and they sell them for $100. The blueprints include plans for both a two- and three-bedroom house, with information on plumbing and electrical work.

It sounds as though they plan to stay around for a spell, and Bob asserts, "This house is never going to be for sale. It has everything we want, so why leave?"

After years of living in conventional houses, they can take a lot of questions—perhaps even a little kidding—if it means that they can live comfortably and quietly out in the country for a lot cheaper than other people live.

MOVE IT

Unwanted houses go at bargain rates—if you have a site.

Until recently, moving a house seemed like a huge, preposterous undertaking, something attempted only to preserve rare historic buildings or to amuse wealthy kooks. Not anymore. Now, a used-house lot in California sells houses to be moved as other lots sell used cars. On the opposite coast, in South Carolina, in a sparsely populated and definitely not wealthy area, six houses have been moved into a ten-mile area in less than a year. A local banker, who arranged the financing of one of the houses, conjectures that house moving is the "coming thing."

It makes sense. For people trying to move from the extravagant practice of disposing of everything from one-use razors to no-return bottles back to the old habits of saving, using up, and making last, the notion of disposing of a house just because it can't be used where it sits approaches total waste. Given the current costs of home mortgages and building, the fee for moving a house comes to far less than building a new one or buying one in a livable location.

Here are stories of two South Carolina families who bought houses cheaply and had them moved to land they already owned. Neither the families nor their houses have much in com-

By Sara Pitzer

mon beyond the moving, except that for both of them, buying a house and moving it was the cheapest answer they could find to a housing problem. The differences in the way the two families managed the entire process illustrate how totally individual each move is, but anyone contemplating a similar move will find useful lessons in the experiences of both couples.

Burned Out

For Steve and Dianne Smith it all began on their son Jason's first birthday, a day he remembers as the day "firemen broke our house." The fire, which started in faulty wiring, burned their trailer to the ground before firemen could do anything to stop it. Understandably shy of moving into another mobile home, Steve and Dianne quickly discovered that with mortgage rates at 15 percent, buying a new house was out of the question, and with the cost of building materials going up every week, building from scratch was beyond their budget too. They were glumly contemplating building the house a little at a time, as they could afford materials (Steve is a carpenter) while they continued to live with Dianne's mother, when Dianne saw the door that changed everything.

She was bicycling near her mother's house one evening after

supper when she noticed an unusual front door on an uninhabited old house. Thinking it would be nice for their new house when it was finally built, she tracked down the property owner and tried to buy the door. He wouldn't sell but did encourage her to go back and look at the sixty-year-old house, which had been his old home place. If she could get it moved, he said, he would sell it for $3,000.

Price for Moving

The Smiths had already figured out how much they could afford to borrow at going interest rates—$20,000—and they knew anything they did would have to stop at that limit. A house-moving company said moving the house the three miles from its old location to the Smiths' land would cost $4,700.

Steve and Dianne decided to go ahead. The house had 2,500 square feet of living space, was basically sound, and almost could have been lived in as it was. They felt they could do the work that needed to be done. If they borrowed $20,000, they thought they'd have plenty left for remodeling. They started to look for a loan.

They seemed like ideal candidates. Dianne is a professional bookkeeper, comfortable with money, able to organize finances, solicit bids, compare prices, and

The Smith house, a bargain at $3,000.

keep track of spending. Steve's being in construction meant not only that he could do much of the work himself but also that he would be able to trade labor with fellow workers for such jobs as wiring which he wasn't qualified to handle.

Armed with this rationale and a detailed accounting of their plans and expenses, they went to the bank. Then to another. And another.

After appealing to five banks, they realized they were in a Catch-22 situation. Savings and loan banks wouldn't lend money for the house until after it was moved, even though the mover was bonded against possible damage and loss, and the owner wouldn't release the house for moving until he had his money.

Finally, a Loan

It took six months before Steve and Dianne finally got a loan from a bank where a loan officer they knew personally decided to bend the rules. "He said later he never saw anyone look as pitiful as we did that day," Dianne recalls. "I think he helped us because he knew it's almost impossible for young couples to afford a house."

While they waited for a loan, Dianne looked for the best prices on every aspect of the project. She got bids from masons, cement companies, and lumber companies. She says, "I must have called ten different places just for prices on a 2×4. I was on the phone constantly for a year."

Next, Permits

Once the loan was granted, her phone time was for calling to arrange all the official permits required in her county for moving a house. These included a movers' permit, a percolation test (which cost $100), a septic permit, and remodeling and building permits. Acquiring all these necessary permissions (which would vary, depending on where you were moving your house) took a month.

With these preliminaries

74

done, the crew began preparing the house to move. They tore off all the chimneys. These cannot be moved. They took off the porch steps and front porch base, which also could not be moved. And finally, the crew took down the lightning rods and disconnected all the grounding wires, then jacked the house up off its brick piers onto irons. All this took five days.

The next step for the Smiths is rarely necessary in moving a house. They had to remove a hill. The house sat on top of a small hill which had to be graded down with heavy equipment so the house could be backed off it and kept level. Then, when the house had been moved from the spot, they had to rebuild the hill to preserve approximately the same topography for the landowner. This expense, which was included in the basic $4,700 moving fee, is one reason the moving cost was so high for a distance of less than five miles.

Moving Day

As the house was hauled down the road, Dianne watched every detail. "After all I went through to get the house, no way I wasn't going to be there when they moved it," she says. Power lines along the way had to be cut to allow the house to pass under; the power company's charge was included in the movers' basic bill. The telephone company did not charge for lifting lines for the house to pass under.

Once the movers had backed the house onto the lot and Dianne had instructed them exactly how she wanted them to

position it, the house was leveled with hydraulic jacks and cement blocks. It was time for the new foundation.

Building the Foundation

The Smiths had planned to dig and build the foundation themselves, but in the first half-day, they found that the red clay and rock on which the house stood had to be dug with a pick. Estimating that at the rate they were going it would take half the summer, they gave up and hired a backhoe and a crew with experience building foundations under moved houses. The digging,

pouring, and building took five men three days and cost $1,200.

The bricks for the foundation cost no more because Steve and Dianne already had 2,000 clean used bricks they had bought a few years earlier for $200. The remaining 5,000 bricks came from the chimneys and porch steps which had been removed from the house before moving. The only hitch in that arrangement was that those bricks had to be cleaned of old mortar before they could be used in the new foundation.

How do you clean 5,000 old bricks? Ask Dianne.

"You beat each one with a

The front hall, roomy and paneled.

hammer till the mortar falls off. And sometimes you give it just one more tap to get off the last little piece of mortar and that'll be the tap that breaks the brick."

Ask Steve.

"It takes a lot of cussin'."

Tapping and cussing took them two long Saturdays and a week of evenings from right after work until dark to clean all 5,000 bricks. Using those bricks, the masons built the foundation all around the house, leaving gaps just large enough for the movers to slide out the irons on which the house rested. After that was done, the masons bricked in the gaps.

A New Roof

With the house now firmly in place, Steve and his brother spent the next two weeks tearing off the old roof, which consisted of a layer of wood shingles and two layers of asphalt shingles. They invited Dianne to help but she decided she didn't like high places. In fact, as far as she is concerned, the entire roofing process was a disaster.

"It hadn't rained in months. We got the shingles half off and it rained without stopping for the next two days," she recalls.

When the rain stopped, it took Steve and another worker just one day to put on the new roof—a layer of plyboard covered with asphalt shingles.

Internal Problems

The rain which fell while the house had only half a roof aggravated a problem inside. Much of the house was walled in old-fashioned tongue-and-groove paneling, some of which had been painted and water damaged, leaving stains which bled through every combination of paint and primer they tried. It took three coats of wall primer, followed by two coats of oil-base paint to cover the stains. Wood which had not been painted ear-

Midpoint in the remodeling of the Smith house.

lier was not stained and presented no problems because they left it natural.

However, ceilings in the master bedroom had been heavily stained by water leaks and the spray finish the Smiths used for other ceilings wouldn't cover the stains. Trial and error led them to applying a layer of Sheetrock and following that with the standard ceiling spray finish.

Wiring

The next major project was the electrical wiring. Dianne says the old wiring might have been usable, even though it was sixty years old, but after having lost one home to a fire which started with faulty wiring, they took no chances and rewired the house. Steve traded labor with his brother-in-law, an electrician, cutting the cost to just the $500 for materials.

The plumbing, on the other hand, Steve decided to do himself, even though he isn't an experienced plumber. "It looks like a maze under the house. Pipes go everywhere," Dianne says, "but the water runs in and out where it's supposed to."

She recalls, however, that they had some problems in the bathroom. They had a four-foot-long tub. All standard tub enclosures are five feet long, so they had to fill in the extra space to make the tub and enclosure match. "And the tub was the only thing in the whole house that was level, but a level tub won't drain, so we had to unlevel it to get the water to run out," she says.

Closing in a small screened-in porch to connect the bathroom

Jason Smith in his carpeted bedroom.

(which had been off that porch) to the main part of the house was managed for just $25 by using pick-up scrap Steve salvaged from his other jobs.

Room Enlarged

Taking out a wall to turn two medium-sized rooms into a large den-dining room was the project that changed the appearance of the house most. They had a stone wall and raised hearth built along one outside wall to accommodate the wood stove, an airtight Blue Ridge Mountain stove which needs to be fed only once about every 12 hours. That is their sole source of heat. (On a cold day the house is cool, but Steve says once the house has been insulated the stove will be more than adequate. Heating is not a major problem in the midlands of South Carolina.)

Steve and Dianne did the work

**"It takes a lot of cussin'."
Steve Smith, on how to clean used bricks.**

77

of knocking out the wall, paneling, and putting up exposed beams themselves. They hired a stone mason to put in the hearth. Putting in the hearth and stove cost $2,000, including the labor for the mason. The beams and light fixtures came to another $140. "We tried to use as much material that was already in the house as we could. We didn't want to buy anything we didn't have to," Steve said.

Kitchen Renovations

In the kitchen their renovations included building in overhead cabinets to expand cupboard space beyond the four bottom cupboards already there. They also closed in one window, reduced the size of another, and boxed over a hole which once accommodated a gas cook stove, to make a space for a refrigerator. This much totalled $200, but the kitchen is not done. There are no doors on the cabinets yet, because the knotty pine Dianne wants costs $60 a sheet, which would bring the cost of cupboard doors alone to $300. "That's enough for a house payment," Dianne said. She's thinking of relenting and settling for painted cabinet doors because she's tired of having the insides of her cupboards open to view.

Next the couple tackled Jason's bedroom. It had had a fireplace which backed against another fireplace in the next room. The chimney, of course, was gone. They closed off the fireplace, but kept the mantle and built bookshelves in what had been the hearth area. They also built a large closet in one

Dianne's kitchen, roomy and bright, after remodeling.

corner of the room. (There were only two closets in the entire house.) And although they have not yet carpeted the rest of the house, the floor in Jason's room is carpeted, in case he should fall out of bed. Costs for finishing Jason's room came to $300.

Money Ran Out

At this point, Dianne and Steve ran out of money. They had expected their borrowed $20,000 to be enough to do all they did plus carpet the rest of the house, install central heat and air conditioning, and insulate the house. Now they are resigned to doing these things gradually, as they can afford to. It hasn't been much comfort, but they understand why their money didn't go as far as they'd expected, in spite of all their

careful estimates and price comparisons.

The first reason was inflation. The cost of materials went up steadily, sometimes *daily*, as they worked. Since they bought lumber and other supplies only as they needed them, each project ended up costing more than they'd expected.

Another reason the money ran out before the house was finished was that they hired help on several jobs they had planned to do themselves. Because they were living with Dianne's mother during the time they worked on the house, they wanted to finish and get into their own home again as soon as they could. When they saw that a job was going to take a long time if they tried to do it alone, they went ahead and paid for extra labor. "You get so you feel like you just want it *done,* no matter what it costs," Dianne said.

Some of the money went to completing projects they had first planned to leave until later, finishing the dining room–den, for example. Finally, Dianne is convinced keeping an open charge account at the lumber company was a mistake. "We'd go down and pick up things as we needed them and in just a month we'd run up a $3,000 bill," she said. She says they would have needed the materials, whether charged or not, but feels they would have done a better job of keeping up with those costs if they'd been aware of how much they were spending.

Celebration

But even with what remains to be done, the house is livable and it feels like home. They moved in the end of August, four months after the house had been moved to their site. And to celebrate being "home," they took off all their clothes and, as Dianne puts it, "ran through all the rooms buck naked, yelling at the top of our lungs—just because we could."

They continue to work steadily on the house, painting, finishing the porch roof, cleaning up the grounds and so on, but compared to the months they spent laboring every day after work until dark and every weekend, what they're doing now seems easy. Sometimes they even take a weekend off. Both agree it has been a complicated, aggravating, and exhausting project. They say they'd never do it again—"unless

there was no alternative." But they also point out that the day they moved into the house it was already worth *twice* what they'd paid for it. That, once at least, makes it worth all the effort.

A House on the Waterfront

When Fran and John Rives decided to buy a house and move it, their motivation was the same as the Smiths—saving money. But there the similarity ends. House moving was simpler for the Rives because they did less of the work themselves and because their house, being newer, required less modeling to make it the way they wanted it to be.

The Rives owned a waterfront lot on Lake Murray, South Carolina, where they'd always

planned to build a home. On weekends they often drove to the lake to look around and dream. But by 1981, when soaring building costs showed no promise of going down any time soon, the Rives concluded building a house on their lot would be impossible and they began looking into other housing possibilities.

Unlike the Smiths, they already were living in a home they owned and could have built a new home in stages more comfortably, but they found it would cost almost as much as building the house all at once. Next they looked at houses for sale on the lake. These turned out to be priced completely out of their range. They looked at houses near, but not on, the lake, which they could have bought through HUD and with VA financing, but they couldn't find anything they liked.

A LOOK AT THE SMITHS' EXPENSES

House	$ 3,000
Movers	4,700
Septic tank	900
Permits	150
Wood heater	700
Carpet	250
Appliances	1,000
Stone work	700
Storm windows and doors	300
Materials	7,800
Labor	3,000
	22,500
Less personal savings	2,500
Mortgage	$20,000

Borrowed $20,000 at 15¼ percent interest for 15 years. Payments $294.12 (includes mortgage insurance on husband and wife).

"I guess we were always thinking too much of the lake to be satisfied with anything else," John said.

And, just as they were running out of ideas, they heard from friends about some people who had bought a house on condemned property cheaply and had it moved. With that possibility in mind, they began looking for a house to buy inexpensively and move to their lake site.

Talked with Mover

There was some question in their minds about whether it would be possible to get a house onto their lot because the road to it is rough and narrow and the lot is considerably lower than the road. Fran contacted a house mover whose name "was an old familiar local name" and he went with her to inspect both a house she was considering and the lot at the lake. He assured her it would be no problem to move a house onto the lot.

But the family hadn't found what they thought was the right house yet. They were simply marking time again when Fran saw a newspaper classified advertisement for a single-story house for sale for $15,000. It had to be moved because the land on which it stood was being claimed for a highway widening project. The house had three bedrooms, one bath, a kitchen with eating area, and a living room, a total of about 1,300 square feet of living space, plus a two-car garage. It was only eight years old. The sale was to include appliances, carpet, and other floor coverings and wall paneling.

Both Liked House

Fran and her fourteen-year-old son, Will, went to look at the house. They both liked it. After learning a real estate man also was interested in the house, Fran decided to act quickly. An hour later she met the seller in a lawyer's office to make a 10 percent down payment on the house. "I thought it would be okay," she said, "because Will liked it and Will usually doesn't like anything."

Sixty days later, the house was twenty miles from its original location, settled on the Rives' lakefront lot, and complete with a new wing. The family had

The Rives house, after move and enlarging.

moved in. Had it not been for the time it took to build the new wing, the family could have moved in within thirty or forty days.

Bricks Removed

Preparations for moving the Rives' house differed somewhat from preparations on the Smith house. The Rives' house had a brick veneer front which had to be taken off. Such veneers won't survive moving. Windows, doors, and cupboards had to be taped shut. And finally, as with the Smiths, power, water, and sewer lines had to be disconnected. All this preparation was finished in one day; actual moving began very early the next day.

The house and garage were moved separately. The Rives were surprised the garage could be moved at all, since it had no floor except the concrete slab on which it had rested and that, of course, was left behind. "I don't have any idea how they managed it," Fran said. "We didn't see any of it. They told us not to watch." So, the moving process Dianne refused to miss, the Rives chose to spare themselves. John said they didn't need the anxiety. "We knew that when the building is lifted and when it's lowered again are critical. Everything has to be kept even or the house will crack. We didn't want to see it," John said.

But twenty miles is a long way to haul a house at a speed not much faster than a person could walk, and inevitably, some other people saw it. Fran's employer stopped her at work that morning and said, "Fran, I think I saw

Will, 14, and his mother, Fran Rives.

your house in the middle of Route 378 this morning. Are you moving today?"

Backwards?

John was first to see the house in its new location. The moment must have caused him some of the anxiety he'd been hoping to avoid because when he got there the garage was facing the wrong way. "I called the movers right away and told them the garage was backwards," he said. "They said they knew it; they just happened to put it that way and they'd be turning it around."

The Rives' sixteen-year-old son, John Paul, had mixed feelings when he first saw the house. He said, "It looked awful funny sitting there with no bricks on it.

SHOPPING FOR USED HOUSES

If you live in California and want a used house, try visiting Tony Lozano's used house lot in Stockton, California. He finds out about houses ready to be demolished, buys them, then moves them to his seventeen-acre lot.

Most of the houses on the lot are in the $15,000 range.

It didn't look like the same house at all."

Before the house could be re-bricked, new foundation posts had to be built under it and the house had to be lowered onto them. A contractor arranged all these details. (A septic tank and well had already been put in.) County laws also required that the foundation be inspected and approved before the house was lowered and the irons removed.

Wing Added

As soon as all this was done, builders began the new wing the Rives had decided they wanted to add for additional space. And instead of replacing the brick veneer as it had been, just on the front of the house, the Rives had the entire house bricked. This meant that in areas not previously veneered, windows had to be firred out to the brick. Also, a crack in the corner of the living room had opened up as the carrier turned sharply off the road and down onto the lot, and this had to be repaired. Then the house was repainted inside and wherever there was exposed wood outside. Much of this was work homeowners *could* do themselves. Fran and John chose not to, although they did put in the lawn and landscaping themselves. John says that in hiring such work it is crucial to have a contractor and labor who can work cooperatively with the house movers and, ideally, who have had experience on similar house-moving projects.

Ready for Occupancy

By September, 1981, the house was ready for occupancy. The new wing transformed the original house into a four-bedroom house with three baths, kitchen and dining area, living room, study, and entry way, a living area of about 1,800 square feet. The total cost of the house, not counting the price of the lot, was between $57,000 and $58,000. John has never broken out the costs of each separate job and item, but he does have specific figures on those aspects of buying and moving a house which would be useful to others thinking of trying a similar project. And he notes that the cost of the new wing, about $20,000, wouldn't apply if one selected a house and did not add on to it.

Original house	$15,000
Moving house	2,800
Moving garage	1,000
New foundation posts	6,000
New brick veneer	6,700
Drilling well	2,300
Installing septic tank	1,300
Total	$35,100

Saved Money

Looking back on their experience, the Rives felt moving a house to their lake site was an excellent idea; there's little they would do differently. "It wasn't cheap," John said. "But it was far less expensive than anything else we might have done."

As for deciding what was the worst moment in the entire experience, John said, "Well, for me, personally, the worst was moving in."

John Rives shows off new entrance to home.

Fran laughed and agreed, "That *was* pretty awful, wasn't it? We moved ourselves. Yes, the day we moved in, that was the worst."

Advice

It becomes obvious from just these two families' experiences that every house-moving project will be a unique undertaking in which the problems and costs will depend on the people, their house and site, as well as their movers and helpers. Some general advice may be distilled from the details.

First, if you are thinking of moving a house, before making any commitments, it is crucial that a *reputable* mover inspect both the house and the site to estimate the costs and to anticipate and discuss possible problems.

Second, it is important that your mover and any contractor or labor you hire be willing to cooperate.

Third, in figuring costs, allow for a few unexpected developments, such as deciding to finish a room you'd originally planned to leave alone. And be sure to figure such things as the cost of grading, topsoil, and landscaping if you will need them.

Fourth, be realistic in figuring how much you can do yourself and how long it will take you. The Smiths' experience suggests that even people experienced in construction can get into more than they can handle in the time they've allowed. And the Rives' experience makes it clear that

having professional help facilitates matters.

Fifth, don't be surprised if the costs you encounter differ dramatically from those in these stories and from those of other people you know. It's the individuality of the project asserting itself again. For example, it cost the Rives less to move their house fifteen miles than it cost the Smiths to move theirs three miles. The difference was in the grading and rebuilding of the hill, requiring extra heavy equipment, to get the Smith house off its original foundation.

And most important, when you begin such a project, be sure you understand what responsibilities are yours and what ones are assumed by the mover. In the case of the Rives and Smiths, the movers carried insurance against damage to the houses and arranged for the permits to cut power lines and move oversized loads over the public roads. Most movers would assume this responsibility, but be sure.

Finding a House

All these cautions are inconsequential, however, if you don't have a house to move. Where can you find one? Not everyone looking for a house to move can pick one out of a newspaper advertisement as quickly as Fran Rives did. And, even in California, used-house lots don't clutter every corner. If the South Carolina banker is right and house-moving is the coming thing, competition for such houses

could become active and, probably, the houses would become more expensive. The plus is that means of matching houses with buyers also would become more refined.

Meanwhile, good beginnings include checking with real estate people, and going directly to areas where a project such as highway widening or a dam is claiming land and forcing people to leave their homes. In the past many such buildings have been destroyed when they might have been moved successfully. If you see a house that seems suitable and it wears no "for sale" sign, look for the owner or the people responsible for the activity going on. Even if the people on the scene have no authority over the building's disposal, they'll know how to find out who does.

Another place to look for houses which might be moved is in areas of the rural countryside where fewer farmers are working more acres. Often farmers are eager to buy land but indifferent to the extra buildings on it. Some might be willing to sell you a house to move even though the idea hadn't occurred to them before.

Nor do you have to limit your prospects to buildings used for homes. A small abandoned church, the shell of a drive-in bank, an old township building, or almost any sound, unused building which no one seems to want where it is could make good possibilities.

Don't be afraid to ask.

TRY LIVING IN THE ROUND

Silos are easy to erect, inexpensive to heat, and sometimes cheap to build.

Alex Howe received a letter from the tax assessor in Bainbridge, New York, advising him to apply for an exemption on the silo being erected on the family farm.

"The assessor was astounded," Alex recalls, "when he learned the silo was to be the residence for me and Marilyn Rice, my bride-to-be."

The Howes are only two of several thousand Americans who have found happiness in houses in the round, or "drums," as they are known in the trade.

Most round houses are prefabricated silos built especially as homes, but some are recycled silage (cow fodder) silos, or drums built from scratch as homes. Most silos are multi-storied and usually have one room per floor. You'll find rooms shaped like a piece of pie in the single-floor structures.

Those who live in silos are loyal to them, and cite these reasons for building and living in one:

- They're easy to erect, even for those untrained in carpentry.
- On a per-square-foot basis, they're inexpensive, costing as little as half what a conventional house of the same size would cost.

By Ray Bearse

- They're economical to heat, if well insulated.
- They're a joy to live in, for those who want something different from the conventional three-bedroom ranch with attached garage.

Those interested in inexpensive housing may find a good deal in a used silo. A lot of them stand unwanted today in dairy country, either on farms no longer supporting a dairy herd, or on prosperous farms where they have been replaced by the bigger metal models.

Buy an Old One

Al Gurney, longtime Unadilla Silo Company sales manager, encourages those thinking of recycling an old farm silo.

"The oldest ones are bleached almost pure white inside, as a reaction from the chemicals in ensilage. It's very pleasant to see, looking like pickled oak. I recommend to anyone who comes across an old Unadilla silo to go ahead and buy it. They are usually still structurally sound and hence very good buys. That way all the new owner needs (to convert the silo to a house) is a bit of basic hardware from us," he explains.

These old models "have a delightful winelike aroma." One

word of caution from Gurney: don't buy a silo that has been treated inside with an asphalt compound such as creosote. The smell will linger forever.

Common in Vermont

The conversion of silos from their former use to homes has been commonplace in Vermont, long a dairy state. There silos are used for such diverse purposes as homes, art galleries, professional offices, the administrative headquarters of a college, a restaurant, ski shop, and ells to conventional houses.

When Harris Peel retired from the U.S. Foreign Service, he and his wife, Margaret, retired to her ancestral home in Danby, Vermont. They converted the barn and silo to an art gallery. The ceiling of the forty-foot high silo "makes a superb place to suspend mobiles," Mrs. Peel says.

Psychologists Robert and Mary Belensky of Marshfield converted a farm silo into consulting offices.

In South Londonderry, Woody's Cracker Barrel Ski Shop—ski shop, store, and fitting rooms—is in twin silos. On the third level are the living quarters. Twin silos, too, were used for offices by Goddard College, in Plainfield, with the president's office located in one of them.

Early Conversion

Ted Scatchard began his conversion of a silo back in 1968, making it one of the first in the state.

Scatchard is a well-known potter, living in East Charlotte. His neighbor, Mark Prindle, had a Unadilla silo, long since fallen into disuse.

"I paid him $125 for the silo," Ted recalled. "I braced it with used 2×4s, then sawed it in half with a Sears saber saw, and removed the top half. That made it possible to move it without removing utility lines."

Scatchard hired a Scott crane—$25 an hour—and moved the top section to a corner of his sixteen-acre meadow.

"The next spring we moved the bottom section. But before moving it, I hired the power company's posthole digger to excavate a dozen postholes. I set a Sonotube—a heavy cardboard form—into each hole and then poured in ready-mix concrete. These concrete posts formed the foundation for the silo."

He chopped four feet of rotten wood off the silo base, then "the crane lifted the bottom silo section into place, then placed the top section on top of it." He was ready to complete the interior.

Three Levels

Scatchard uses the base level for storage, the second level as a kitchen-studio, and the top level as a bedroom-living room.

Since erecting the silo he has added an eighteen-foot square room with conventional walls, a room that features a large (and second-hand) Thermopane window.

With the exception of putting that window into place, and moving the silo, Scatchard has done all the work himself.

The cost? "If you include the original cost of the silo, bracing, moving, re-erection, concrete, lumber—mostly salvage—and wiring, I have just about $1,000 invested," he explained.

Buying a New Silo

For those ready to spend a bit more and start with a new silo, there's a fairly well-established route to follow. Write to the Unadilla Silo Company, Unadilla, NY 13849, send a check for

Ray Bearse Photos

The Scatchard silo, with bedroom-living room on top.

Ted Scatchard and his works.

$10, and ask for their current information packet on silo houses. Unadilla is the only firm left manufacturing wooden silos, and the only one offering them as homes. Prices start from about $2,500, and range up to more than $12,000. After studying the packet, you can decide what you want for size, height, roof style, and number of openings for doors and windows. Given this information, the factory will quote a price for you.

The factory will furnish interior wooden nailing rims at the proper levels, to support the floor or floors in multi-level structures.

The company advises several foundations are possible. These include circular concrete pads, a concrete base ring sunk below the frost line, and individual concrete posts such as Ted Scatchard used. Cellars are possible. The building kit includes Y-shaped angle irons to tie the wooden silo base to the foundation.

Some purchasers build and install their own windows and doors; others purchase standard models such as Andersen. Unadilla will make the necessary door and window cuts, or the purchaser can do this.

Construction is fairly simple. The stave material, untreated eastern spruce, has two metal dowels about eight inches from either end. The dowels lock into corresponding holes. After the unit is up it is bound together with steel hoops.

Avoid Creosote

Farm silo staves are often treated with creosote, but home builders do not use this smelly material. A good stain will last indefinitely; some leave the exterior, and sometimes the interior, untreated.

The company suggests several methods of insulating. The most expensive one is to buy two silos, erect one inside the other, and insulate between them. A more conventional method is to put up interior studs, put insulated batts in place, then finish the interior as you would a conventional house.

Putting up a silo kit is a task that can be approached with some confidence by the person who is not a master carpenter, but who has had some experience with tools. Many of these silos are owner-erected, and often the construction is the first carpentering the builder has ever attempted.

Did Own Work

In Marlboro, Vermont, Louis Audette did most of the work on his three-level silo dwelling. He is a onetime United States Information Service official in North America, and once he was a lecturer in anatomy at the Yale Medical School. Audette said he had some volunteer labor to help him—and he was brave enough to design and construct an exterior enclosed semi-circular stairway.

"I got the idea," Louis said

about his silo home, "from looking at various farm silos. A friend mentioned that the Unadilla Silo Company would make custom cuts in their standard silos. I wrote them a letter and received an enormous package of design drawings and descriptions. They supply drums of any size upwards of about fourteen feet in diameter and just about any reasonable height. They have a shavings silo at their factory which is thirty-five feet wide and seventy-five feet high. They make a number of roof shapes and supply rings for supporting floor joists. They do not make windows, stairs, or dormers, but they will advise you on the best and/or most economical way to build them.

Built Model

"My wife, Anna, and I looked their stuff over. At that time—1970—about 400 silo homes had been built, though none of the design was as complicated as ours. We built a cardboard scale model and drew up our ideas which we presented to Albert Gurney, then sales manager of Unadilla. He corresponded with us, offering suggestions on materials and money-saving methods including a method of cutting our slit window frames into the actual staves.

"Our negotiations were capped by a trip to Unadilla. This was not essential but it was certainly fun. We closed the deal for two drums. The first floor was sixteen feet in diameter by ten feet high. The second floor drum was eighteen feet in diameter by twelve feet high, with a gambrel

Audette silo, built from scale model.

roof. This roof with four dormer windows gave us a third floor. I added the dormers. I got extra staves for the exterior stairwell. Unadilla made all the hardware in its own shop.

"The *Whole Earth Catalog* in those days pointed out that it is much cheaper to make a window

that lets in light or air but not both. It was right after the New Haven riots. We had access to a lot of broken plate glass for free. The pieces weren't very big. I could get all the glass I wanted but no pieces were more than four inches wide. That was in character with the silo shape. I

88

Narrow windows flood Audette silo with light.

put in little doors for ventilation. The problem was how to set the slits into the staves, but Al Gurney of Unadilla came up with a practical, easy, and inexpensive solution.

Students Helped

"As to help, I had some city rubes (his Yale graduate students). There is nothing more stressful than setting up a weekend plan—it took nine actual weeks to build the house but those weeks were stretched over a year and a half of weekends and vacations. Twelve helpers would arrive all with the same tool, a hammer, when there was need for but three or four hammers."

Louis thinks the cardboard scale model was of considerable help. It was large enough so that it eventually ended up as a playhouse for his children. It was designed so that the roof and other major segments could be removed.

The cost—excluding beer for the volunteer help—of the entire house was about $4,500.

In the dozen or more years since Audette built his home, hundreds have followed his footsteps, with Unadilla reporting silo homes in at least thirty-one states, from Maine to California and from Oregon to Florida. Yet

they're surprisingly different, with every owner and builder creating variations that fitted individual desires.

Beer Barrel

In Kennebunkport, Maine, Richard and Nancy Blomgren have a three-level residence they've named "The Beer Barrel." Upper levels have a two-foot overhang, making it a round garrison home. While most silo homes have one room per level, these Swedish-Americans divided the first floor into four quarters, providing a living room, bath, kitchen, and dining room. The second level has two

89

The Blomgren 'Beer Barrel.'

for his family. The Pate silo has a sleeping loft, with the main floor having a living room, kitchen, and bedroom. Pate attached a more conventional ell to the silo. It houses a bedroom and bath.

Custom-Built Models

Ranging the widest in design, appearance—and price—are the silo homes that are custom built.

High above the ski resort village of Stowe, Vermont, is the custom-built silo of Kenley Squier, CBS Sports Spectacular announcer, his wife, Susan, and their two children. They didn't build the home, didn't even think of living in the round, but were house-hunting ten years ago.

"We came upon this house accidentally, when we came to look at the house next door. We loved the looks of it, found it was available, so we bought it, even though many people tried to discourage us.

"From the beginning the kids loved it. My daughter said, 'This is a castle.' "

This is how Susan Squier, tall and blonde, describes how she and her husband bought the round home they have lived in and enjoyed.

Five Stories

The house is five stories high, towers forty-four feet in the air, and now has a three-story rectangular ell.

There's a host of rooms in all that space. The house has storage space and laundry units in the basement, children's bedrooms on the second and fourth levels, a kitchen and dining room on level

equal-sized bedrooms and a large bath. The top level is a second living room.

This, the first silo dwelling in Maine, was co-financed by the Maine Housing Authority, the Maine Savings Bank, and the Veterans Administration.

J. David Pate put up the silo for the Blomgrens, and was so intrigued by it that he erected one

three, and a music room with four windows at the top level.

There's a garage and Jacuzzi on the first floor of the ell, with a living room on the second level—the same plane as the drum's third floor—and a master bedroom and bath on the top level. The enclosed stairway is attached to the outside of the five-level drum, while the ell has an interior stairway.

"It hasn't always been this way," Susan explained. "When we moved in the top floor was the living room, which, as you can see, has a spectacular view. But it was too inconvenient. You had to run down two floors and then back two flights just to get a glass of water."

Popular Room

And now, "This level, the third, serves us as kitchen-dining room-living room. Even though we now have a separate living room in the new section, this is still the room where everybody congregates."

That third-level room is round (and twenty feet in diameter) on three sides, and flat on the fourth. The flat side provides the space for the kitchen. The west side has a large Thermopane glass wall, and a sliding door opens onto a spacious sundeck. Exterior stairs lead to the lawn below. A wide doorway opens into the new living room.

Feared Troubles

Susan expected some troubles when they moved in.

"Our son, when we moved here, was not yet two. I had or-

Children call the Squier silo a castle.

91

dered accordion-type gates for the stairway entrances, fearing he might fall downstairs. When they arrived, none of them fit. He learned to go up and down stairs from the day we moved in. We've never had an accident."

She also feared that she wouldn't hear the children at night if they cried, since they were several levels away. "The intercom I had ordered hadn't arrived when we moved in. The first night here I heard him cry, and I was downstairs in a flash. I have never had trouble hearing them, so we cancelled the order for the intercom."

There have been problems:

"One of the problems right off was slivers. It is all rough side lumber. I got slivers continually for a matter of months. Then, somehow, we just didn't get slivers anymore. We learned how to approach the house."

Susan admits, too, to wishing there was "a bit more room. We live here in this third-level kitchen: three dogs, two children and a husband who, when he is home, has a lot of business calls. It's a bit crowded."

But there's an advantage to five levels. "Living on levels like this makes for far greater privacy than living in a conventional house."

And, summing up, Susan says, "To me, it has always been a joy, slivers notwithstanding. This house has a personality of its own. It's comfortable. It's casual."

LOOK AHEAD

Higher initial costs can be offset by lower operating costs.

If you aren't up to building your own home but dream of finding a new energy-efficient house, the key may lie in locating the right builder, one whose vision goes beyond making money.

Rational Alternatives, Inc., of Santa Fe, New Mexico, is such a construction firm. Founded by the unique combination of two philosophy professors (one a woman) and a logger, Rational Alternatives (RA) is developing a remarkable solar community based on a common vision.

Duty: Functional Housing

"We believe our primary duty is to see that any structure designed by us functions well," they write in the RA prospectus. (How many builders have you met who think in terms of duty?) "Emotional or aesthetic expression in a home should not interfere with the fitness of the building to fulfill its purpose—a durable and comfortable living space warmed by the sun. Simplicity, purity of design, sound construction, and practicality are ideas which express our functional approach," they add.

Talk of form flowing from function in a house may evoke images of metallic boxes, ugly lines, and bare pipes. Yet nothing could be further from the reality

By Linda Lindsey

Heat is stored in the stuccoed concrete walls.

of El Dorado at Santa Fe, as the Rational Alternatives community is known. By relying on traditional southwestern pueblo-style architecture, which has developed precisely to fulfill a function, the builders achieve maximal thermal efficiency while retaining aesthetic appeal and plenty of creature comforts. The RA homes we visited were warm, livable, and quite elegant. At the same time they were priced for moderate income families. And the builders are working to bring down costs even more.

The principle of simplicity is expressed in the direct-gain solar design employed in all the homes in El Dorado. Space heating is provided by solar radiation passing through large south-facing windows into the living space where it is stored in the thermal mass of the walls and floor for later distribution. In this type of house/collector or collector/house, enough of the sun's warmth can be retained to meet 70 to 80 percent of normal heating needs with no external power, according to Patricia Conkling, wife of Mark Conkling, RA vice president (former philosophy professor at NM Highlands).

93

South-facing windows provide 70% of the space-heating needs.

Concrete Absorbs Heat

All the RA homes built thus far are completely passive except for the domestic hot water systems. This means that heat flows through them by entirely natural means: no whirring fans or groaning motors, nothing to break down. While the exterior walls are of cement block, all the interior walls are composed of real adobe bricks, some of them plastered and some with rough surfaces for better heat absorption. The floors are of dark green or brown concrete that collects heat too. Embossed with "things that look like giant branding irons," they are finished with a wax that requires little care, says Helen Wilson (the other philosopher). It takes a close look to discern that they are not actually Mexican tile.

The heavy mass stores enough heat to last through several overcast days, even though Santa Fe experiences few of those. Strategically placed windows provide for the entry of fresh air and set up a circulation system that brings the warm air stored in floors and walls to all parts of the house. "Sun scoops," or reflector skylights, provide an additional source of indirect light and heat in some rooms.

Nestled among the mountains of northern New Mexico at an altitude of 7,000 feet, Santa Fe has a temperate climate, with cold nights but mostly warm, cloudless days. It is rated at 6,000 degree days. This puts it on a par with Ohio or Pennsylvania. Thus the basic design employed by RA would be appropriate in more northerly locations with enough sunshine (insolation around 200).

Buyers Satisfied

All this sounds very fine in theory, but, you may ask, do the people who bought RA homes really like them? We talked with Gloria Dobek, who, with her husband, Andrew, moved to El Dorado in 1980.

"When we retired here from Austin, Texas, we wanted to avoid a tract house like the one we had lived in," says Gloria. "We wanted openness, a place to do organic gardening. We were aware of New Mexico being in the forefront of solar activity, but hadn't thought much about solar. It was when we heard about the cost of utilities here that we got interested. We are very happy with our choice."

The Dobeks first looked at older homes closer to the center of Santa Fe with an eye toward retrofitting, but concluded that costs would be prohibitive. They talked to several solar builders and after comparing approaches, they liked the simplicity and maintenance-free aspect of RA homes. "Some solar homes aren't really solar, we discovered," Gloria says. "They may have as much glass on the north as on the south." The home they purchased is bermed with earth three-quarters of the way up the north wall, with only one small window in the kitchen.

Never having lived in a solar home, the Dobeks didn't know what to expect. They asked a lot of questions, and found the builders straightforward and informative, providing complete information about the operation of the house.

"It's so sensible," says Gloria. "The sun comes in through the windows on the south. Since the house is long and narrow, the sun will cover three-fourths of the floor space during the coldest part of the winter."

It heats up the embossed concrete floors which Gloria finds "very appealing after living in a shag rug place." There are no cold drafts because the house is sealed tightly and cabinets or closets line the north wall. The only work occupants have to do is pull the Mylar shades at night to keep the heat in, or during the day if they want less sun. When the temperature dips to zero or the wind is very strong, insulated draperies (optional equipment) may also be drawn.

"The walls do retain heat," Gloria says. "It's warm in the off-seasons, spring and fall, which seem to be the hardest times for solar." In fact, the house stays so warm at night that the Dobeks often open the bedroom windows.

The builders will customize each house within the confines of the basic design and the budget of the buyer. The original plan for the Dobeks' house, under construction when they first saw it, called for the solarium or sun room to be on the west side. Because Andrew likes to get up early, however, it was moved to

"Lining the north wall with cabinets is a common-sense way to provide storage space and insulation at the same time."

Gloria Dubek

Log vigas dominate the ceiling of living room.

must be too large. Since there is no room on the roof for another collector, the solution may be to get a smaller tank, and be satisfied with less but hotter water.

The hot water heating systems are not built by Rational Alternatives, Helen Wilson assured us. "We've tried several different commercial systems without finding one that is entirely satisfactory," she says, "so we're now trying to develop our own design."

The Dobeks like the roominess of the walk-in closets and the kitchen pantry. "Lining the north wall with cabinets is a commonsense way to provide storage space and insulation at the same time," Gloria points out. "I don't understand why all the builders don't do it." In this scheme the residents' clothing becomes part of the insulation.

Tax Credits

You can't get a tax credit for closets as insulation, but most other solar aspects are eligible, according to RA president Bob Gibbens (the logger and housing contractor). "The solar tax credits now available make both active and passive systems economically attractive," he says. In the past the solarium and the active domestic hot water systems have been options, but now, because of the tax credits, they are included on every home. "The consumer ends up paying less than half of the cost of a $3,000 hot water system. That's a bargain," Gibbens surmises.

The Dobeks had no trouble with financing, as they had just retired and could put 50 percent

the southeast corner, where they now enjoy breakfast each morning.

Not Enough Hot Water

On the roof of the solarium are perched the collector panels for the domestic hot water system. Interestingly, this active system is the only aspect of their home

with which the Dobeks are not satisfied.

The two panels do not provide enough hot water without using the electric back-up, which they are loathe to do. "We have to shower in the afternoon, right after the sun goes down, if we want enough hot water," Gloria laments. It seems that the over-sized eighty-gallon storage tank

down. They closed out their 16.5 percent mortgage by selling their home in Texas within a year. The market price of $86,500 was high compared to what they could get in Texas, but average for Santa Fe, even without the savings on utility bills.

Back-Up Heat

The previous winter Gloria spent with her daughter in a "regular house with an uninsulated roof" and was "never so cold." So she was quite impressed with the warmth of her new home. She never expected that the utility bills would be quite so low; not in her wildest dreams did she imagine the sun would do all her heating. Yet the Dobeks never once turned on their electric back-up heat. They did, admittedly, use their fireplace some, but it was a very cold winter. "If you pay no heating bills, you can afford to have higher mortgage payments," Gloria points out. "And cutting your own wood is a good way to keep in shape."

Solar Community

Although the housing market is depressed nationally, Rational Alternatives homes are being sold as soon as they are built. In fact, the builders are so encouraged that they are turning El Dorado into the largest solar community in New Mexico, if not the nation. Forty homes have been sold thus far and RA is developing 214 units on 450 acres, including greenbelts. Restrictive covenants require each home to be at least 50 percent solar. Because RA has bought into the already existing El Dorado development, many elements of a community already exist, including a fire department and security patrol, swimming pool and tennis courts, and even a solar elementary school with classrooms for 250 students.

"Rather than having a simple aggregate of people one might loosely call a 'neighborhood,' we would like to see a community of folks who share interests concerning energy-use, life-style and recreational pursuits," they say. Of course, being located out in the wilds twelve miles south of Santa Fe makes El Dorado a place distinct from the city of Santa Fe. It means that views of the Jemez mountains to the west and the Sandias to the south are unobstructed. Lot sizes range from one to four acres, there are few through streets, and most of the lots are on cul-de-sacs. Yet it is only twelve minutes to the nearest hospital, half an hour to the cultural attractions of Santa Fe.

Cutting Costs

But is it low-cost housing? Prices of houses built to this point have ranged from $65,000 to $95,000, not counting the "Total Solar" photovoltaic house unveiled in February, 1982. It came in closer to $200,000. Size (1,000 to 2,000 square feet), and

The solarium is also used as a breakfast room.

owners' tastes have a lot to do with the prices, and RA is constantly seeking ways to keep prices down. "Passive solar homes are normally quite expensive, as are all-adobe homes," says Patricia Conkling. "Our design combines efficient passive solar with functional pueblo-style architecture using some adobe. And the price is lower than comparable houses, on the average."

Concrete blocks filled with concrete and coated with urethane insulation on the outside, then plaster, are cheaper than real adobe bricks. And the embossed concrete floors are an inexpensive way to provide heat retention in combination with an attractive surface. Everybody hates concrete floors—except these. Helen Wilson says that RA is looking into the possibility of using slump block for all walls in order to reduce the cost of plastering. "A third of the labor cost of a house can come in plastering," she complains.

Options

On the other hand, there are many touches of luxury in RA homes that the builders resist giving up. These increase the cost. Hard rock maple is used for countertops and islands in kitchens, oak for the cabinets, while the hand-crafted cabinets lining the north wall are of pine or ash. Mexican tile is a must in kitchen and bath. "It can cost as much as $500 for tile setting in a kitchen," Helen says. The style, price, and extent of tile may be determined by the buyer, however. Kiva fireplaces, insulated

drapes, skylights, and built-in benches or "bancos" are options that most owners choose. But they are not necessary. According to Helen, "We look forward to building $50,000 homes for people who share the concern with energy-conservation but have limited budgets."

Large Lots

Lower-cost houses could be placed on the smaller, less attractive lots. Currently a lot will run one-third to one-fourth of the total cost of a home in El Dorado. The Dobeks' 1.5 acres, furnished with utilities, would have sold for $20,000. Part of the reason for the large lots, though, is proper siting for solar. One requirement of a direct gain home is that the structure face south. This prohibits typical neighborhoods of rows of houses facing the street. RA solved the problem by placing homes on the rear, or north part of a large lot, leaving the front a practically untouched, private space studded with pinon and cedar trees.

Lower energy costs also make these houses more affordable. Not everyone has saved as much as the Dobeks, but almost. Since all the homes have separate meters registering the daily, monthly, and annual consumption of electricity for space heating, RA has been able to verify the success of the basic design. Twenty of the all-electric passive solar homes consumed an average of 331 kilowatt hours for heat during a 12-month period in 1980–81. At the rate of 7¢ per kwh, that came to $23.17 for the year, paid to Public Service Co.

of New Mexico, which provided the metering.

For those for whom energy independence is more important than cost, RA is building homes powered by photovoltaic cells on the roof. The "Total Solar" home is, they say, the first privately financed attempt to provide all electricity as well as heat from the sun. It is based on the same direct-gain passive solar design. In addition to wood heat back-up from the fireplace, back-up is provided by an active water system that, through a heat exchanger, heats air that is circulated through ductwork. Cooling can be achieved, too, when necessary, with an evaporative cooler employing the same ductwork for distribution. The active solar hot water storage tank also provides hot water for domestic use as well as for the hot tub.

Exchange of Electricity

The active solar systems, as well as lights, stereo, and appliances in the 2,300-square-foot home, are powered by an array of photovoltaic cells rack-mounted on the roof. A flat reflector at the foot increases the amount of radiation striking the solar cells. The system includes DC to AC power conversion equipment connected into the public utility grid. Conscientious owners using the energy-efficient appliances should be able to avoid paying any charges to PSNM, which provides power when the sun is not shining. By selling power during the day, they actually make their electric meter run backwards. Peak output of the system is about three

Here's the only window in the north wall, in the kitchen.

kilowatts in bright, direct sunlight.

The Total-Solar house was designed by Steven J. Strong of Solar Design Associates of Lincoln, Massachusetts, and is based on a federally subsidized house he designed in Carlisle, Massachusetts and a prototype built by

RA with federal funds at Las Cruces, New Mexico. Thus there is plenty of research behind the venture.

Still, building with solar cells on speculation is a daring deed in the housing industry. RA's courage was quickly rewarded. "We had a big opening for the Total-

Solar house, with busloads of people coming out from Santa Fe," says Helen Wilson. "And, lo and behold, one of them bought it the first day."

How to find innovative builders who know what they are doing? Now that Rational Alternatives has expanded, it has received much publicity in the media. But it began as a small, obscure group with an ideal. State and local solar energy associations as well as alternative technology research institutions such as Ecotope (Seattle, Oregon), New Alchemy Institute (Woods Hole, Massachusetts), and departments of architecture at universities are in touch with the latest advances in home building and the people who are applying them. *Solar Age Journal* and *Shelter Magazine* are good sources too.

But be sure to talk to home owners themselves before putting down your money. What seems like a "rational alternative" on paper may not stand the test of four children and a dog.

MAKE THE MOST OF YOUR ASSETS

It's a sure way to save money when building your own home.

Nancy and Jeff Small made use of all their assets when building their home in Charlotte, Vermont.

The list was long:

- *Land.* They'd been given a five-acre lot as a wedding present.
- *A tractor,* used for lumbering—and very helpful when they were clearing their lot.
- *Family and friends,* who gave of their time, energy, and support to get the house built.
- *Jeff's job* with a heavy machinery rental firm that also owned a hardware store.
- *Access* to Garden Way construction books. Nancy works for Garden Way Publishing.
- *Skills.* Jeff had done fine carpentry on boats, understood home construction, so could do much of the work, and knew how to contract for the remainder.

"And, most of all," remembered Nancy, "a real desire to have a house." The couple had lived in five places within a year, and were living in a lakeside cottage, uninsulated, when they began construction in Septem-

By Roger Griffith

Nancy and Jeff Small did much of their own work.

ber—with the threat of a cold Vermont winter looming over them. "We worked, every single minute we had, from September to January," said Nancy.

Worked Fast

Each one of these assets helped them to build better and at a lower cost—and (that threat of winter) much faster than they thought possible.

Result was that in February they moved into a two-story structure, a home on the second floor, a spacious garage-shop for Jeff's construction business on the first floor, 896 square feet of space on each floor, for $30,000, including well and septic system—or $15,000 less than they had estimated for construction by a commercial firm.

It took some doing. "We didn't do the chimney and masonry, Sheetrocking (we could have done this, but wanted it finished as quickly as possible), concrete work, the well, and some of the electrical work," Jeff said. That work was contracted for. They did all the rest.

The two builders can now look back on their project and with some dispassion decide what they did right, and what they will do differently when they build again.

Careful Planning

"We planned carefully," Nancy recalled, "and even built a rough cardboard model. This gave us a three-dimensional look at what we had on paper. It helped. For example, we changed the pitch of the roof on the basis of this."

Careful planning, too, went into their site selection, picking a spot that blended with other uses for the property in the future, siting the house to give them shade and a woodland view in the summer, a look at Lake Champlain in the winter.

They're proud of the passive solar advantages of their home—big windows massed on the south side, and topped by five large skylights. Window quilts will blanket all these windows, for less heat loss on wintery nights, and less sunshine during the warmest of the summer.

Six inches of insulation cover the walls, with double that amount on the ceiling.

The heating system works

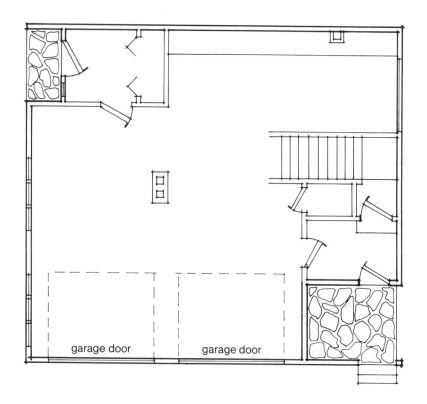

Above, floor plan of first floor shows air lock entrances and large open area for shop. Below, the living quarters in the second floor. Dotted lines indicate location of three large skylights in living room-dining room.

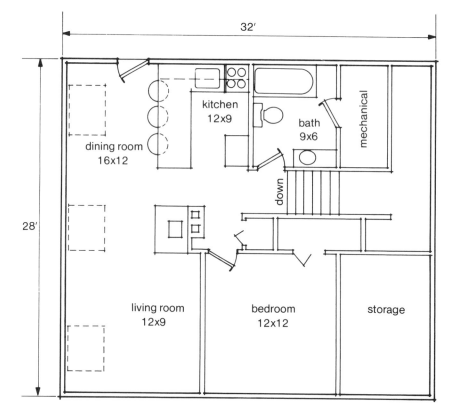

well, providing all the heat they need at low prices. In Jeff's first-floor workshop, an airtight wood stove burns all winter. Much of this heat flows to the second floor, so the stove there is used only occasionally. The Smalls installed electrical baseboard heating, for backup. They haven't used it yet.

Nancy likes the heavy beams across the living-dining-kitchen area. They enhance the feeling of space—"and the plants love it up there." The Smalls feel, too, that they have gotten the most from their living space by making the living room, dining area, and kitchen into one open area. A bedroom and bath complete the home.

If they carry out their plans eventually and build a house linked to their present building, they'll do some things differently.

"We would start early on all of the planning work—the loan, building permit, preparation of the land, things like that. All of those things took much longer than we had expected, and delayed the actual start of con-

Erik Borg

Nancy and Jeff have breakfast at kitchen counter.

struction until September," said Nancy.

They were prepared for long hours of work—and found out it was even more work than they had expected. Jeff left his job in January and worked full-time on the house, and even then the house was "just livable" when they moved in in February.

They wouldn't do that again, they agree. It causes problems. Furniture is in the way. There's a tendency to get accustomed to such things as molding not yet in place, bare boards that must be stained or painted.

"It's easier to go to the house to work," Jeff explained. "That way you can leave a mess, when you're in the midst of a job. You can't do that when you're living in a home."

A feeling of anxiety is created when you're living in a home, and it never seems quite done. "Spend an extra month and get everything finished," advises Nancy.

Ready to Build Again

Unlike some couples who found home-building too much work, the Smalls haven't cooled on construction. Quite the opposite. Nancy likes the satisfaction of working with her hands, so different from her desk job as a sales management executive at Garden Way Publishing. And Jeff has gone into construction full time, with a growing business.

What's next?

"Right over there," Jeff points. "That's where we'll put up a barn to house some of my construction equipment."

RAISE A WORK CREW

Eight children helped build the Andregg home.

Linda Lindsey Photos

Carol Andregg admires family-built home.

Doing it yourself is easier if you have a lot of help. In the case of Carol and Perry Andregg, there were eight children to provide labor. The Andreggs have been working together for four years to make a new farmstead for themselves. Every member of the family has participated in the construction project, from the "baby," Heidi, 5, to Perry Jr., 19.

"Actually, we didn't have much choice in the way we went about it," says Perry. "It had to

By Linda Lindsey

be a labor-intensive project because we didn't have much money." The Andreggs spent most of their savings on forty acres of land peppered with sagebrush and rocks on Redlands Mesa above Hotchkiss, Colorado.

This move represented a new beginning for the family, an adventure that brought everybody together. They had always lived in rented housing, moving frequently, never having a place they could really feel at home. Finally Perry and Carol tired of moving and were determined to

get a home of their own. They took the big leap when they found a plot of land that was inexpensive because it was unimproved and had no irrigation water.

Well Costs $1,700

The first item of business was to locate drinking water. Since other folks in the area had successfully drilled wells, they were fairly confident of finding water. Still, it was a relief when the well came in after 115 feet of drilling and $1,700.

After the well there was water but no funds left with which to build a house. How were they to manage? They had no previous building experience and no materials. There were too many of them to live in a tent. Undaunted, Perry gazed out at the barren expanse of land and said, "Well, we'll just have to use what we've got—strong backs and plenty of rocks."

Found Materials

They began to gather the makings of the house wherever they could. Carol took a paper route covering many miles of rural countryside. Every time she noticed a pile of junk or an abandoned house she would inquire if the owner would like to have it removed free of charge. In this way she located two houses that the family dismantled to provide

105

lumber, roofing, windows and doors, and even nails for the new abode. Farm auctions were also a source of many building materials, as well as fixtures and furniture.

Preparation of the site began with the clearing away of the sagebrush and rocks. This operation was accomplished with hoes and shovels—and the little ones picked up rocks by hand. Luckily, the ground was flat. They couldn't have afforded a bulldozer anyway. Because Carol and Perry had full-time jobs, they worked on weekends and evenings during the summer. The result of a couple of weekends' work was a huge pile of stones with which to start the foundation.

Perry stepped off a basic

Carol recalls collecting stones for house.

All of stones came from the building lot.

106

shape—a rectangle forty by fifty-eight feet—and placed stakes in the ground, stretching string between them. Then, before he could do any cement work, he had to prepare his water source. A cistern—actually, a concrete septic tank—was buried underneath what was to become the front porch and a pump was hooked up to bring well water into it for storage. Then Perry could begin to mix mortar in an old galvanized tub and to lay up the foundation.

The house was framed with salvaged 2×4s on sixteen-inch centers. A shed roof with a very slight pitch was then constructed with 1×6s and 1×12s on top of 2×6 rafters. A black felt cushion for protection against hail was tacked on next, followed by roll roofing.

Rocks—and More Rocks

Once the framing was completed the family took on the major task of the project: rocking up the exterior. First the house was wrapped in plastic. Then six inches of rock were mortared on the outside. With the aid of the older children Perry mixed every bit of the mortar by hand, keeping the ratio of cement to sand at one to four—"a good hot mix" he calls it. He kept the mix as dry as possible in order to make a stronger set.

The rocks are medium sized, four to six inches in diameter. Remnants of Colorado's volcanic era, they are basalt, the same material the Hawaiian Islands are made of, only so old that they are weather-worn grey instead of black.

The children would be sent out to "round up the rocks." Janina, 18, or Nick, 16, would push the wheelbarrow while the others (Dell, 14, Gene, 13, Tabatha, 11, Buffy, 8) would walk alongside, throwing in rocks as they went. When they finished a load it would be brought back and dumped at Perry's feet to be washed and readied for incorporation into the wall. "We must have fifty tons of rocks in the place," Carol says, "and it all came from right out there. Why, if there was a market for rocks, we'd be rich."

Perry laid up the rocks as fast as he could. "I didn't have much choice," he says. "Those kids just kept hauling in rocks and I had to do something with them." As the wall got higher it became more difficult to heft the rocks up to lay them in the wall. At one point a chain was formed of children, from smallest to largest, to hand buckets of rocks up to Perry, who was perched on a ladder. Finally he had to build a tripod-based hod carrier to hoist the buckets up to roof level.

"We did all the work ourselves," Carol, a plump, vivacious woman with a quick smile, says proudly. "The first year we didn't even have electricity. By the time we got it, we'd already done most of the hard part." Two wheelbarrows and a pickup truck were worn out hauling rocks and cement. Hooking up to electricity made possible the use of a Skillsaw for the interior work, speeding up the carpentry considerably.

If you visited the Andreggs' home you would never guess how it was built and how little money went into it. The finish work is done with care and good taste, and that's what people see, after all. No one would dream, for instance, that the house is insulated with plain, old cardboard.

Cheap Insulation

Insulation is expensive these days, Perry realized, and although he wanted a tight, warm house that would withstand sub-zero temperatures and frigid winds whipping across the mesa, he couldn't see paying the current price for fiberglass. He searched for an alternative material that was cheap and readily available . . . and came up with cardboard boxes.

Carol started looking for boxes on her paper route, and soon they had accumulated hundreds of them. After spraying them with a borax solution as a fire retardant, they tacked two layers of them between the studs in the walls.

The first year the Andreggs had brown cardboard walls. It wasn't the most pleasing wall covering, but it was warm. Eventually they managed to purchase some particle board which they nailed over the insulation and painted white. On the ceiling the cardboard is now covered by acoustic tile.

What's the insulating value of cardboard? "Who knows," answers Perry. "If it's all you can afford, it's what you go with. It seems to do fairly well, actually. We've lived a lot of different places and we've never been warm before."

The Andreggs congregate near fireplace.

"If there was a market for rocks, we'd be rich."
Carol Andregg

Warm House

"It's a real warm house," Carol agrees. The neighbors come by, she says, and can't get over how warm it is inside a house built with plain, old rocks and insulated with cardboard. Of course, most of them don't realize what it's insulated with. All they know is that it's not breezy like their houses. Those stone walls are thick and tight. No drafts can get in to put a chill on things. And once they get heated up, the rocks stay warm.

In fact, the Andreggs installed two stoves, a Franklin fireplace in the living room, and a Fisher stove in the dining room. But if they fire up both of them, they have to open a door or window—unless, of course, it's 20° below zero. Then they're thankful for all the help they can get.

Solar Heat

The rocks are not the only element that keeps the house warm. Solar heat is important in the performance of the house too. The passive design Perry dreamed up involves big windows on the southeast corner. Glass can be a very expensive item in the construction of a house, unless you can manage to find a "special deal." The An-dreggs obtained their solar windows from a trash man while visiting relatives in Arizona.

Carol, always with an eye out for materials, noticed the windows sitting in a truck full of junk next to a condominium construction project. "They were in a truck that looked like it was on its way to the dump so I asked what was the matter with those lovely windows," Carol says. She was told that they were being disposed of because of a ripple in the top portion of each window. "I looked at those windows and I could hardly see the ripple, so I offered to take them off his hands." After being carefully hauled back to Colorado, those windows now provide a wonderful view of the Ragged Mountains.

The four windows are three feet wide and six feet tall. That makes a lot of glass to admit light and heat. Two are installed in the living room and two in the front sun porch. The curtain Carol made covers the top foot of the window containing the ripple.

The Andreggs were lucky in one respect. Facing the house toward the county road produced the proper orientation for solar heat as well as for the view. They didn't want a funny-looking house facing the wrong direction that would contrast with the surrounding farmhouses. Their finished place is interesting but not striking. The rocks blend well with the countryside, and the solar aspect is not really noticeable.

Low Ceilings

Another important feature affecting the thermal performance of the house is the height of the ceilings. It is not a tall house. "I

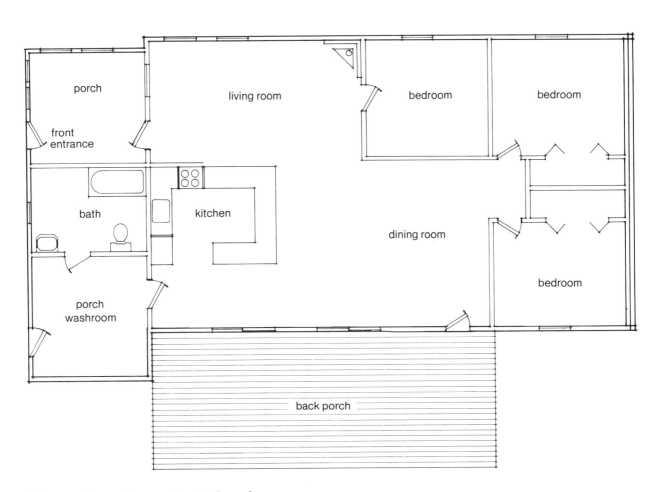

Three porches are featured in this floor plan.

109

would never go over seven feet in a ceiling," Perry says. He attributes much of the house's warmth to the fact that the air does not stratify much when the ceilings are low. Also, the doors, which Perry made out of particle board and 2×4s, are heavier than commercially made doors, and better insulated. The Andreggs have caulked and weather-stripped all openings, as well.

When asked for advice about building a low-cost dwelling, Perry replies, "Don't build too big." As it stands now, the Andreggs' house has three bedrooms plus two sleeping porches, a living room, dining room, kitchen, and bath. Their approach has been to build what they require now and to allow for expansion. As the children get older they will add on. The first addition will involve closing in the back porch to provide bedrooms for the younger children who, as they grow up, will need rooms of their own. As the older ones go off to school or to work, others will take their places, so that only a few rooms will have to be added.

Scrounging

Carol's advice is predictable: "Scrounge," she says. She is a master at the art of finding the right thing to fill a need. Her living room floor, for example, is covered with carpet samples gleaned from the auction of the estate of a rug salesman. Nearly a hundred of them are tacked down to form a crazy-quilt carpet. One advantage of this approach is that any color of furniture goes with the carpet. If

Carol decides to change her color scheme she doesn't have to rip up the carpet. In addition, any stained or discolored pieces can be replaced.

The kitchen is full of other indications of the Andreggs' ingenuity. Shelves are made from a bed taken apart, for instance. And pots and pans are hung from a railing taken from an old school bus.

Perry would like to improve the safety factor of the house. Although he was very careful to put in insulated stovepipe through the roof while installing both stoves, he has experienced chimney fires and knows how fast they can burn your house. To decrease the risk of fire he used rock to make the wall on either side of the Franklin fireplace in the living room, and put a brick

pad underneath. Still, he worries and thinks that the only way to relieve his mind would be to place the heating unit outside the house in a separate structure and pipe the hot air in under the floor through ducts.

Second Roof

What problems have been encountered since the family moved in two years ago? Perry says, "The tarpaper kept pulling the roofing nails out, so I had to put on a second roof." This involved nailing a series of 1×12s on top of the roll roofing and covering them with "tin" (corrugated aluminum). The double roof provides additional insulation and the metal reflects heat in summer.

A potential problem lies in the

Kitchen is center of activity.

110

placement of the plastic wrap. Since the Andreggs attached it to the outside of the framing members, warm, moist air from inside the house will cool around the framework and the moisture will condense. Enough of this and the studs can be wet enough to start to rot. Plastic is usually placed on the interior to avoid this.

Root Cellar

At the same time they were building the house, Carol and Perry were thinking about other aspects of self-sufficiency. A root cellar to store food for the winter was a high priority item. The same building methods were used in the cellar. They dug out a big hole with picks and shovels, hauling the dirt and rocks away with a wheelbarrow. The cellar would have been entirely underground, but they hit a hard layer of gypsum at three feet below the surface, and that was as far as

COSTS	
Land	$12,000
Well	1,700
House materials	4,000
Cement	400
Septic system	750
Total cost	$18,850

they could go. Some of the rocks dug out were used in the four-foot thick walls of the cellar. Those thick walls help to maintain a uniform temperature of about 50° F. throughout the year.

Food stored in the cellar is from their own garden, which is watered largely by grey water. To take care of their toilet wastes, they installed a septic system and a leach field, again using home-grown rocks. But water from the showers is run back onto the garden. "We just couldn't make do if we had to try to sprinkle the garden with well

water," Carol says. Even with using showers instead of a bath and recycling the grey water, they have to limit the size of the garden and plant intensively, in order to make the most efficient use of the water they have.

Some of the well water also goes to the animals. Although, as Carol laments, they can't have a "real farm," they are keeping a milk cow and a flock of chickens and plan to get a few goats. The cow barn and chicken house are made of—guess what?—rocks, too.

Food production is a family affair. Even the little kids can help in the garden, while the older ones take their turn milking the cow. The children are proud of their role in building their home and providing for themselves. It is an experience few people have these days.

START FROM THE BOTTOM

Cellar living saves time and money.

Like many owner-builders, Bonnie Macleod and Craig Reeves knew the task of building their own home would be a prolonged commitment. For starters, neither of them had any building experience; they knew they had to keep their fulltime jobs in order to afford the construction costs; and, during the second year, their first child was born. Now, after three years of building, they have an "almost-finished," 3½-story home on sixty-two acres.

To juggle so many demands would have been impossible had they not planned on setting up housekeeping in the unfinished cellar. Two years of cellar living saved them time and money; it also allowed them to grow with the house as it grew around them.

"In retrospect," says Craig, "we wouldn't have done it differently. When you slowly live and think, day in and out, you get perspective; changes come to you—things you never thought of when working on a design of your fantasy—but I wouldn't recommend it for the impatient."

Moving Up

Bonnie and Craig are finally living on the first and second floors. To get there has taken real

By Mary Twitchell

determination, beginning way before the first nail was driven.

Three years after Craig and Bonnie moved to Vermont from city life in Boston, they were still living in an apartment while she worked at the University of Vermont in the zoology department as an electromicroscopist and he worked as a mobile mechanic. They pinched pennies except for buying the gasoline it took to search for property.

"We wanted to spend around $5,000 for the land, which at $500 an acre meant we were looking for approximately ten acres," says Bonnie. "We looked at anything and everything in that price range, but after two years of looking at puckerbrush, swamps, and north-facing hillsides, we realized we would have to broaden our options; we either had to pay a higher price per acre or look at larger parcels. Of course, we wanted the ideal piece—quiet, half-woods and half-pasture, with a southern exposure—something that suited us. When we saw this lot, we bought it in three days. We saw it the first day, walked the boundaries with the Realtor the second; on the third it was ours." They knew enough to add a rider to the agreement contingent upon finding water, but before they bought the land they never had a "perc" test nor their soil analyzed.

These tests aren't essential be-

fore buying most parcels of land, but Craig and Bonnie's land is a triangular piece with its apex meeting the town road. Because the land rises steeply from the road, the number of house sites with easy access to the road was severely limited. Had the soil been unsuitable for carrying the load of the house or not porous enough for a leach field, they might have had expensive problems.

Picking the Site

Bonnie explains, "There is a level area right near the road. We thought about that location for quite a while, but the land is always wet. It would have been difficult to drain. Higher up from the present house site was a second potential location, but the land is full of ledge. We never really considered where we are now. It was hard to see a house site through all the trees and prickers, but once we had the soil checked and the trees felled, it became perfectly obvious. Now I can use the damp, flat area for a garden, but we were lucky there weren't more complications."

Percolation Tests

Percolation tests are simple and must be done before any rural site is considered for a house. A "perc" test determines

112

Craig Reeves admires his handiwork.

mining the soil strength or bearing capacity in the area of the foundation. Stable soil is essential whenever steep slopes are considered for building sites. Soils of vegetative matter, dumped earth (loose fill), or weak clays are unsuitable for foundations, particularly on sloped land. Soil maps and evaluations are available by consulting with local soil conservation, extension, or university services.

Craig and Bonnie took out a small mortgage to buy the land, which is a beautiful hillside piece overlooking the Champlain Valley, with two of the state's largest mountains in the distance. On a clear day the 180° sweep is breathtaking—well worth the two-year search.

Behind the house are the beginnings of a gravity-fed sugarbush—a bonus they discovered after they had purchased the acreage. "We actually had homemade maple syrup last year," says Bonnie, obviously proud of the speed with which she is picking up country skills.

Owner-Builder Course

Craig and Bonnie enrolled in an eight-week owner-builder course taught one evening a week for two hours. Bonnie was still pinching pennies. "You know, being a couple, we could go for the price of one, so I signed up immediately."

In the course they discussed different kinds of insulation, ventilation, energy-efficiency, house orientation, roof slope, and various construction materials. The class next focused on house de-

the soil's capacity for absorbing water. If there is no town sewer system, a percolation test is needed to find the best location for a septic system.

The test is done by digging a hole, filling it with water, then measuring the time it takes for the level of the water to lower. Clay soils, for example, retain moisture, which means the water

passes through the soil very slowly.

Tests should be made in several areas before any house site is abandoned. Sometimes a band of gravel or sand can be found through which the water will pass.

Bonnie and Craig had not checked soil maps. These maps are particularly helpful in deter-

sign. The text they followed was *Designing Houses* by Les Walker and Jeff Milstein. "We'd go home from class," said Bonnie with a laugh, "and spend the rest of the week drawing bubbles."

Planning Sequence

Bubbles are Walker's way of studying spatial relationships. He suggests you list your needs by rooms: their purpose, size, light requirement, personality, special oddities (i.e., noise from large tools), and what room(s) they might adjoin. Each of these rooms (activities) then becomes a colored paper disc. If an activity can go on concurrently with another, the bubbles overlap; if they can only partially accommodate or must exclude one another, the location of the bubbles reflects that. Such diagramming makes the home builder think just how tolerant he will be with someone welding in the kitchen or practicing scales in the workshop.

Next, the possible relationships between activities are explored by moving the discs around different traffic patterns. Rooms can open off a central corridor, or they can fan out at either end of a corridor, or they can be clustered off a central communal area; and they can be stacked (i.e., two- and three-story houses). Once the room relations are tentatively worked out, the house is sited on the land to check how the arrangement will relate to the outdoors. Siting the house makes the owner-builder consider southern and northern light, exposure to weather, view,

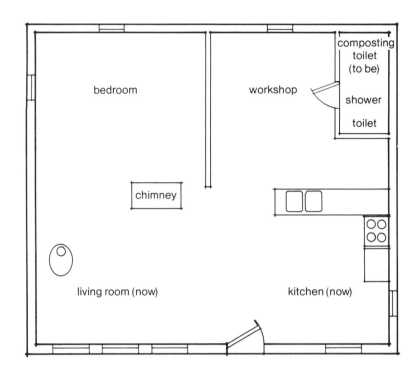

Cellar

access to power lines and existing roads, prevailing winter winds, possible noise, location of shade trees, summer breezes, exposure to neighbors, ventilation, and the impact of house shape on the landscape.

Building Models

"Talking about these things gave us a handle on terminology, materials, and important site considerations as well as more knowledge about what we wanted. But the best part," says Craig, "was the Saturday workshop. That was when we started constructing cardboard models of the layout."

To further explore shape, they cut out three-dimensional models from tagboard and glued

them together. This method allowed them to study different exterior shapes (three-story, ranch, L-shaped) and different roof shapes (barn, gabled, saltbox). From there, they moved to larger models made from corrugated cardboard. They erected walls, cut out doors and windows, added exterior walls and one side of the roof. The other side was removable. With this model they could study the arrangement of rooms—decrease or enlarge them, open skylights, add or delete greenhouses.

More Models

Next they located the model on a large piece of paper on which the view, the path of the

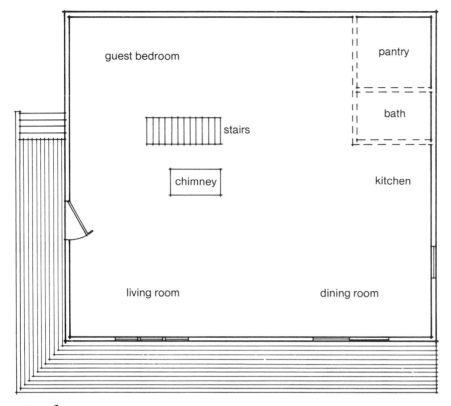

First floor

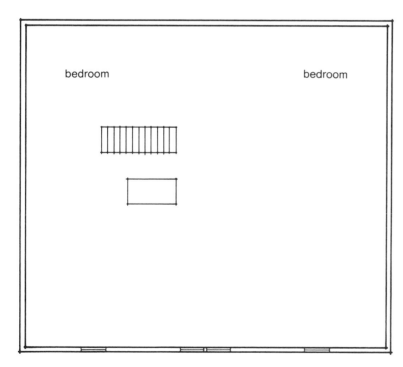

Second floor

sun, and the direction of summer breezes and winter winds were drawn.

The course ended in October, but Bonnie and Craig, not ones to rush into anything, made cardboard models all winter. "We'd build a totally energy-efficient house," says Bonnie, "then realize it was just a box—and how boring. We knew our house had to be practical and energy-efficient, but also it had to be something we could fit into."

They both agree the course was inspirational; it also provided them with an extensive bibliography of relevant, up-to-date carpentry manuals. "We'd read something or see something or come up with another way to change the space, and we'd be back to building another model," says Craig, exhausted just thinking of the time the two of them spent on preliminary designs.

Finally they had a plan on which they could agree, a plan for a 26×30 house, two stories high, practical, energy-efficient, and most livable. They were ready to build.

Craig's father had just retired. This gave them a third pair of hands, and they had saved enough money to get them through the first phase of construction. They had the land and the plans; it was time to move the first shovelful of dirt.

The Cellar

Bonnie and Craig subcontracted the footings and three of the cellar walls, but not without deliberation. Initially they were going to lay up concrete block walls (about one-quarter the cost

The many-windowed top floor.

are stacked without mortar. Once the wall reaches the required height, it is plastered with a special cement.

Surface bonding has proved stronger and more waterproof than the conventional block wall construction. "But," Craig asks, "have you ever seen any block wall that hasn't cracked?"

Given their location with the house tucked into a steeply rising hillside and the fact that they wanted an earth-bermed foundation, the construction of the cellar was crucial. The walls had to be moisture-proof, and block walls even with surface bonding are still more likely to develop leaks and are more susceptible to damage caused by the settling of frost. For these reasons they decided on professionally poured, continuous concrete walls.

Bonnie and Craig weren't taking any chances. "We had the backhoe dig two feet below the footings," explains Craig. "Then we tamped the earth to the footings and added crushed stone and drain tile. The tile was placed holes down and sloped gently away from the house. At each of the tile joints we wrapped tarpaper around the pipe to keep the joints from clogging with silt. The tile was then covered with six to eight inches of gravel. We even had the land behind the house carved and backfilled with stone and sand to be sure run-off ground water wouldn't collect behind the dam we were building. We also put down four inches of crushed stone (which we leveled with a snowplow) before we poured the concrete slab."

of concrete foundations, poured professionally).

Traditionally the footings are poured, projecting beyond each side of the wall one-half the wall thickness and eight inches thick. On top of this the concrete blocks are laid with ⅜-inch mortar joints.

Concrete block walls require no formwork, and the modern variation of surface bonding is even faster than conventional block construction, particularly for the amateur. The first course of blocks is set in mortar (as with conventional block construction), but thereafter the courses

Taking No Chances

The walls were moisture-proofed with a coat of asphalt waterproofing and insulated with two inches of blue styrofoam. Bonnie says, "If we read of ten things, any one of which you *could* do to moisture-proof a wall, we did all ten!"

On three sides, the cellar windows are just barely visible above the earth, which is banked up to within three feet of the first floor. The south wall is totally above ground, has large windows, and had to be something special.

Slipform Walls

Bonnie and Craig erected the south wall themselves using the slipform technique for stone foundation walls. Their method incorporated elements of hand-laying a stone wall, except that the wall was laid up between forms and then backed with a pour of concrete. They faced the wall with fieldstone taken from the land. Sandwiched in between the stone and concrete inner wall are two inches of styrofoam insulation, giving a fourteen-inch wall.

The process of slipforming is economical and simple. Forms are built of 2×3 or 2×4 stock faced with 1×6s which are spaced ¼–½ inch apart. These forms can be made to any size; usually forms eight feet long by eighteen inches wide are about what two people can manage. The forms are placed on top of the footings on either side of the wall. They are held vertically in

place by nailing a top brace temporarily to facing forms. Wire (23 gauge or larger) is slipped between facing 1×6s, twisted, and held in place with bent nails. Further bracing is done with 2×4s nailed to stakes, then

pushed against the forms on either side to insure that the wall will be plumb. Other slipforms are bolted above and/or beside the first form, then braced.

One by one the fieldstones are laid against the wall of the form,

Craig and young Alexander check the masonry work.

and concrete is backfilled around them. When one level is completed and the concrete has set, the forms are "slipped" up the wall for the next level.

This is the slowest, the most satisfying, and the most economical method of wall construction. Usually the stone is from the land, and the forms are used again and again. The only real expense may be your muscles. Builders advise you to be careful to lift with your legs, not your back, and place the larger stones near the bottom where they are easier to work with and will look better.

"There's a small bit of quarried sandstone up in the corner—just for color," says Craig, conceding that all the stones ex-

cept that one were taken from the land.

Provides Heat

Through the three double-glazed Thermopane windows set into this fourteen-inch southern wall, the heat streams into what was their temporary living room, with much of it being retained by the walls.

By the end of the first summer, the driveway was in, 350 feet of wiring had been laid underground to the house, the leach field for the septic system was laid, the cellar wired, the plumbing fixtures installed, and the cellar was liveable. Although living underground was not the ultimate dream of Bonnie and Craig,

they did precisely that for two years.

Comfortable Cellar

In such a space, cellar living was no hardship. Sitting around the wood stove talking, with classical music in the background and sunlight streaming in the south windows obfuscated all clues that this was a cellar. And there were all the amenities: kitchen sink, toilet, shower, stove, and refrigerator. But there were telltale signs: the cellar windows, the concrete floor and walls. And there were suggestions of temporary living: the six inches of fiberglass insulation in the ceiling and the framing for the cellar stairs. But there was little else to suggest that they were living in the future root cellar, laundry, workshop, and mud room. If only temporary, it still felt like home.

The "living room" had a sofa and chairs arranged around the wood stove which was provisionally hooked up. The stovepipe went through one of the basement windows, with an exterior elbow resting on a couple of concrete blocks and the vertical run of the stack somewhat precariously wired to the deck railing. They agree it was less than a five-star stove installation, but it kept them warm (they burned between one and two cords of wood that year), and it sufficed until Bonnie and Craig built the rest of the chimney.

The Upper Floors

The second year they framed and sheathed the rest of the

house. It includes a kitchen, dining room, living room, bath, and guest area on the "real" first floor; bedrooms on the second; and, peaking out the east roof, a third-story crow's nest. It may be the hardest room to get to, but from there you can see over the mountain tops.

Everything except the basement floor and walls is wood frame construction, along with some priceless (because they were free) gems from the dump. The north-south girder of the 3½ story structure is made up of 2×10s. "Whenever I go dump-picking," says Craig, "I always come home with a truckload, but nothing as good as these 2×10s—150 feet of them, nail-free, rot-free, and straight!"

Picking at the dump has provided Craig with many cast-off materials, but as the economy worsens, the competition increases. "It's getting more and more difficult—now everyone's doing it."

Barn Beams

The north-south girder is supported in three places by barn beams, another extra taken from an old barn just for the hauling. "We wanted stud walls," explains Bonnie, "but liked the interior feeling of post-and-beam construction. This was a way to compromise."

The downstairs living room.

119

Owner-builders learn to scrounge for supplies in salvage yards, auctions, and dumps, and to wait until windows are on sale or secure them second-hand when buildings are being torn down. Recycled materials can substantially decrease the financial burden of building.

Help!

"At first we really didn't know what we were doing," Bonnie confides. "Day and night we studied carpentry manuals and I was always on the phone. Paul (the teacher of their owner-builder course) was endlessly supportive. Whenever we ran into structural problems I would use him as a resource person. Then I discovered Milo Moore of the university Extension Service. He was incredibly helpful. I would give him the spans; he would reel off the lumber dimensions and spacing we should use, and he never used a calculator," says Bonnie dumbfounded. As a postscript she adds, "and he wasn't a toll-call away."

There are many good carpentry manuals for the owner-builder. Friends and neighbors, particularly if they also have built, are good sources of information and will be of great assistance when the time comes for raising the rafters. And lumber-yards have certainly dealt with owner-builders many times before.

The "Facilities"

Some decisions which Bonnie and Craig made were dictated by local code. Even though Bon-nie points to the northeast corner of the cellar and says, "That's where the composting toilet will go," they had to compromise with the sewage codes. "Our soil is not good for a leach field, and the well might go dry. They always do around here in a dry year, but local codes don't permit non-water toilets. Maybe someday," says Bonnie. So far their plumbing is traditional ceramic.

The Well

Bonnie and Craig went two years without a proper well. Finally they had a back hoe dig out a reservoir. The well is eight feet deep and lined with three-foot well tiles. So far it hasn't run dry.

Mistakes?

Did they make any mistakes? Bonnie allows that there is great wisdom in agreeing that on the first day of construction the plans thereafter will remain unchanged. They changed their minds—once.

Partway through they decided they wanted a concrete block central chimney. No footing for it had been poured, and to pour one meant first cutting away some of the concrete cellar floor.

Craig explains, "The worse day of my life was digging the trench for the underground wiring—an eighteen-inch ditch in rock! But this was the second worst day. I had a carbide tip on the chainsaw to cut through the floor. There was concrete dust all over—in my ears and nose. My mouth tasted like chalk, and I felt nauseous for days after—never again!"

Once he had sawed through the slab, Craig had to dig out for the footing. Few people will realize how complicated it all was, now that the footing is in and the chimney has been laid up with openings for stovepipes on the first and second floors.

Bonnie still maintains that it wasn't *really* a mistake, deciding at a late date on placement of the chimney. Originally Craig wanted the cellar for an auto

EXPENSE SHEET

Cellar:	
concrete	$1,050
bulldozer & gravel	1,000
labor	2,000
Driveway	1,200
Well	600 (labor)
Culverts	200
Plumbing	276
Septic system	1,037
Wiring	500
Materials	3,540
Total cost for liveable cellar space:	$11,403
Estimated cost for completion:	18,000
Estimated total cost:	$29,000

Heavy insulation throughout the house spells heat savings.

mechanic shop. Because of the possible danger of fumes and fire, he decided to use a detached building. A central flue then seemed logical.

"I think it's best to make plans and not to change them," Bonnie says, understating the obvious.

Easier and Easier

The house has been an extended challenge, especially since Craig and Bonnie had so much to learn. But it got progressively easier. Installing windows, putting up rafters, laying concrete block, building stud walls are repetitive tasks.

"The first rafter is always the hardest," says Bonnie. "We took time out the second year to build a storage shed. It was a good project for teaching us how the rest of the house would go up. We not only developed framing skills, but discovered difficulties we might encounter later. It was an invaluable experience."

Bonnie and Craig can speak to the drain of so intense a project. It was two years before Craig read his first non-fiction, non-building book.

And such an undertaking is stressful on a relationship. Both people come with different (or no) skills. They learn at different speeds, and they're working with each other day and night on a task which is using up their resources—physical, financial, mental, as well as emotional.

Craig and Bonnie agree that certain things were essential to their success. First, they took off part of the second summer. "It's important to pace yourself. Take vacations when the process gets too much, particularly when you're like us who have already been at it for four years. It *is* a strain," says Bonnie.

"And secondly," Bonnie adds, "we were never penniless."

They did take out a small loan to help pay for the land; they also had a small energy loan, given in amounts up to $4,000 for energy-saving home improvements. More important, they saved what they needed before the next phase of construction began. And both of them had flexible employment schedules so that during the most intense part of the construction they were spending three days earning the money to spend in the next four. "Without jobs," Craig says, "it would have been impossible."

To be emotionally and/or financially overburdened usually leads to settling into a half-finished house forever. Craig and Bonnie have avoided this pitfall, but it has taken commitment and perseverance.

What Next?

There's still some trim around the windows to finish on the first floor and some Sheetrocking on the second floor. And then there's the garage Craig wants and . . . the greenhouse Bonnie wants and . . . maybe solar hot water and . . . insulation for a root cellar in the basement and. . . .

It's hard to believe they have learned so much in such a short time.

121

TEAR IT DOWN

Get your house materials at bargain rates.

It seems a shame, even a crime, but many fine old houses and buildings are torn down. Sometimes a building needs too much work to make revamping financially feasible. Often it is impossible to reconstruct an old building to meet modern demands; if the building is not architecturally important, it is razed to make way for an efficient, barrier-free structure.

Other times a building stands in the way of "progress." Progress is often not very progressive; yet, it marches on, and objects in the way get steamrolled into oblivion. Superhighways, urban renewal, and industrial and commercial development determine the fate of many a humble dwelling.

Some buildings are torn down for logical reasons: they are structural invalids, they have been severely damaged by fire or other natural forces, or they are eyesores. Frequently, it is better to start over.

There are, then, various reasons why buildings get torn apart. Society's needs change, and its structures, too, must change. What all this creates is one usable commodity:

Salvageable Materials

When building materials are not wasted, razing is not waste-ful. The materials are simply relocated. They are given new life, new purpose. When materials are recycled, I feel much better when watching a building being torn down.

Instead of a contractor carefully tearing out materials, transporting them, storing them, advertising them, then selling them, it is best if there's a person available who wants and needs the materials and is willing to remove them immediately.

Is this person you? If so, you can acquire used materials cheaply—perhaps for nothing besides your time.

Finding a Building

A good scavenger keeps his eyes and ears open at all times when searching for usable salvage. Frequently a good scavenger will learn by word of mouth about a barn that's being torn down or a house that's being cleared away for another parking lot. Often you'll see promising buildings when driving from place to place. Let people know what you're looking for and information on good prospects will come your way soon enough.

If you need materials quickly, then active searching is in order. Contact salvage yards and salvage companies and ask about upcoming projects.

Fire-damaged or long-abandoned houses are potential sources for used material. Contact the owner of a building to see if a mutually beneficial deal can be worked out. Owners of abandoned buildings can be found by calling the city tax as-

By Alan D. Roebuck

SALVAGE GUIDE
MATERIALS IN A HOUSE

Worth saving	May be worth saving	Not worth saving
Lumber (joists, beams, etc.)	Insulation	Shingles
Doors	Siding	Dry wall
Windows	Kitchen cabinets	Wiring
Plumbing fixtures	Flooring	
Bricks	Heating unit	
Built-in furniture	Stairs	
Subfloor	Pipes	
Plywood	Carpeting	
Ventilators	Flashing	
Mantels	Flue liners	
Gutters and downspouts	Metal roofing	
Finish trim		
Door knobs and hardware		

Worthless? Not to ace scavenger Alan Roebuck.

sessor. The owner's name and address are public information. If you are interested in several buildings, go into the tax assessor's office and examine the tax rolls yourself. The tax assessor may be reluctant to give you too many addresses over the phone.

Once a Building Is Found

Each situation requires a different approach. Rarely will an owner allow you into his house to strip out only what is desired, leaving the building partially dismantled. Usually the entire building must be torn down. Partially dismantled buildings are dangerous. Children attracted to the site could be seriously injured if the structures were to collapse. For the children's protection, for the owner's protection, and for your protection, *complete* your salvage project.

To assure success, come to an agreement with the owner defining your involvement in the razing project. If you plan to tear down the entire building, decide exactly what the process will involve. Will you haul away extraneous materials? Will you leave the site clean? What will you do with the basement cavity?

If the building is within city limits, you will be under city jurisdiction. The process of razing the building will be a city concern—not just a matter between you and the building owner. Most cities have regulations stating precisely how a razed site will be left; this is for everybody's protection. Be ready to comply with these regulations.

Generally cities demand that the building be razed completely within a reasonable amount of time. You may have to erect a temporary fence to keep the

youngsters out of the area during demolition. Generally all rubbish must be removed from the site. The basement is most often not considered a satisfactory receptacle for trash; it must be cleared of all scrap. Often the only thing left will be the foundation walls. And the city may inspect the site. After the inspection, the basement cavity is often filled with sand or other clean fill. Then the site is left clean and level. It is neither an eyesore for the neighbors nor a dangerous area for curious youngsters.

Permit Required

Complying with these regulations will reduce some of the profits of scavenging a building. Permits to raze buildings are often required, and this is another added cost. So understand exactly what you're getting into

123

before consumating an agreement with a building owner.

When you must haul away all unwanted materials, hire a person with a dump truck and a backhoe to remove them from the site and from the basement cavity. This same person can bring in sand fill for the basement and can smooth the site to finish the job. This will cost between $200 to $350, or about the price of one good bathtub. If you can save that much through salvaging one item from the house, such as the bathtub, this pays for the contractor who cleans up the site. The other materials you can regard as a bonus.

Reaching an Agreement

Once the building has been found and the city requirements have been determined, it is time to negotiate an agreement with the owner of the property. To avoid misunderstandings, this agreement should be in writing. Who will obtain the permit (if one is needed)? When will demolition begin? How long is it to take, approximately? Will there be an insurance policy written so the owner is not liable in case of injury to you or anyone else? Will it be totally up to you, the salvager, to comply with the city's desires? Will you be compensated for tearing down the building?

The latter is a definite possibility if you are going to rid the neighborhood of an unneeded or condemned building. If the owner had to hire a company to tear down the building, it could cost $800 or so, depending on the size and complexity of the job. But it is going to take you longer than it would for a bulldozer operator. Since it will take longer, the owner is open to more risk. And since demolition is not your normal line of business, there is a greater potential for things to go wrong—another liability for the homeowner.

An equitable way to work out these problems is this: agree to take care of all facets of the job—including getting the permits, calling for inspections (if and when needed), lining up the contractor to remove rubbish, and filling the basement to city specifications. Then ask the owner of the property to pay only your actual expenses. This way the owner saves several hundred dollars. The project costs you nothing, and you obtain all the materials free. You donate your time, and you receive a ton of building materials worth as much as $7,000. The owner takes a slight risk, gets his house torn down, and saves hundreds of dollars.

If you can swing this kind of deal, you are on the right track toward successful scavenging. Some owners, though, may want to know exactly what the job is going to cost them—instead of leaving it open-ended. If so you assume some of the risk, which is still fair. You must estimate accurately how much you will spend on the job before you give the owner a price.

To estimate accurately the expense you will incur, determine exactly what you must do to comply with all ordinances relevant to razing a building. Consult the city building department and learn the cost of all permits. Ask a contractor what his charges will be for cleaning up the mess and filling the basement with sand. Then add another $150 or so to cover unexpected expenses. With this figure, you are ready to approach a homeowner and enter into an agreement.

The Written Agreement

A written agreement does not have to be complex. "Legalese," the language of attorneys, does not have to be included to make something legal. A written agreement should contain the date of the signing, a description of exactly what is to be accomplished, the house address, the starting date for the project, the dollar amount to be paid for completing the job, and the payment schedule.

When drafting the agreement, leave out ambiguous language. Phrases like "a prompt and timely fashion" are too vague and open to interpretation and dispute. Don't state "each and every detail will be completed," since this is also open to debatable interpretation. Does "each and every detail" mean topsoil will be spread about and seeded with grass? Spell out the terms of the agreement clearly and succinctly. Have a witness to each signature. Here's a sample agreement of the type that I've used.

Tools

At this point, you have covered all of the preliminary bases.

LETTER OF AGREEMENT

On this day, 21 February 1983, be it known that Henry Houseowner, owner of 2159 Easy Street, agrees to the demolition of 2159 Easy Street by Sam Salvage of 368 Live End Road. Sam Salvage agrees to begin demolition by April 1, 1983; agrees to complete the work in a timely fashion without undue delay; and agrees to obtain the necessary permits from the City of Lost Way, which has jurisdiction over the 2159 East Street property. Salvage further agrees to comply with the regulations of Lost Way concerning the demolition of the building at 2159 Easy Street. The building site at 2159 Easy Street will be left clean of debris and will have the basement area filled in with sand, as required by the City of Lost Way. The foundation walls will remain intact. All materials taken from the razed building will be the property of Sam Salvage. It is further agreed that upon completion of demolition of 2159 Easy Street and upon certification of compliance being issued by the City of Lost Way for the job being completed in a satisfactory manner, that Sam Salvage shall receive the sum of $425 (Four Hundred Twenty-five Dollars) from Henry Houseowner as payment for the removal of the building at 2159 Easy Street and for complying with the regulations of the City of Lost Way regarding the demolition of the property at 2159 Easy Street address.

The above agreement has been read and is fully understood. I agree to the above terms.

_____ Date_____ _____
Witness   Henry Houseowner

_____ Date_____ _____
Witness   Sam Salvage

You have the agreement, you've obtained the permit, and you understand what you are to do. Now it is time to assemble a few tools.

I've had tremendous luck finding good tools at flea markets. Sometimes tools that are no longer made can be found, too. Often used tools are better than new. So, if you don't mind a slightly worn look, hunt around at flea markets and garage sales and see what you can find.

Only a few tools are essential. Generally speaking, the bigger the tools, the better they work. But, if finish trim is to be salvaged, a variety of sizes is necessary.

The most important tool for scavenging is the *nail puller*. It makes for quick, clean, and easy work, and it leaves materials in good shape, so they don't lose their value. A nail puller has a handle that slides down on a shaft, forcing the teeth of the puller into the wood. This clever tool is available for about $20, and you don't have to salvage many boards to pay for it.

Another necessary tool is a *power bar*. Power bars are hard to find, so sometimes you will have to have one made by a welder. A power bar weighs about fifteen pounds and is five feet long. The shaft is round, and one end has a chisel-type point.

A solid, round bar of steel could be ground down at its end to make a simple power bar.

Power bars are helpful for breaking away unwanted materials. By forcing the long, heavy bar into an object and leaning on the bar simultaneously, a strong, destructive force can be developed. For more gingerly tasks, you can make a lighter bar by welding together a hollow steel pipe and a flat piece of steel for the blade. The lighter bar won't be strong enough to pry all materials apart; if too much force is exerted, the hollow pipe will bend.

Crowbars and *flat bars* are two other necessary tools. Generally, two different-sized crowbars are needed; one about eighteen inches long and another thirty inches long should suffice. A flat bar looks like an elongated "S." It is made of a flat piece of steel and it has claws like a hammer but smaller. A flat bar can be pushed into a tight space without ruining the edge of a piece of wood. This is especially helpful when removing trim. Inexpensive, small flat bars, only six inches long, are also available. These are useful for removing finish trim without defacing it. Flat bars are used with a hammer. For example, they are pounded into the space between the trim and the wall.

A good *claw hammer* will also be needed. The claws have different curvatures; the straighter claws work the best. A straighter claw can get into tight places. Steel-shanked hammers often have straight claws, and they are much more durable for pulling

Tools of the trade include, from left, bolt cutters, sledgehammer, coal shovel, flat bar, nail puller, crowbar, and reciprocating saw. At top, a power bar, and at bottom, a push broom.

nails than are wooden-handled hammers.

If electricity is available, a power saw will be very helpful. The best one for demolition is a reciprocating saw. Several different blades can be inserted into the saw, making it useful for cutting through a variety of materials such as wood and metal. This is helpful since many of the boards to be cut will be laced with nails.

A reciprocating saw has advantages. A circular saw requires room for the saw housing, but the reciprocating saw's blade protrudes, making it ideal for reaching into tight places. You can obtain blades up to nine inches long that will cut through a wall in a single cut.

In lieu of a reciprocating saw, a *circular saw* with a carbide-tipped blade will do. In fact, even if you have a reciprocating saw, you should have a circular saw. Circular saws cut quicker and straighter than reciprocating saws, making the circular saw ideal when there are no space limitations. A circular saw with a carbide blade can cut through several layers of shingles and through the roof sheathing, too.

A large but cheap pair of insulated *bolt cutters* will also come in handy. These are used to clip electrical wires, and can be used to clip nails as well.

The rest of the tools you will need are perhaps obvious: a *sledgehammer*, *screwdrivers* of assorted sizes, *pliers*, a *hacksaw*, *wrenches*, *vise grips*, and some *rope* in case you have to tie something up or bring something down. Bring along a *push broom* and heavy-duty *coal shovel* for clean up.

Safety Equipment

So, you have your array of tools and you're all ready to head out and start tearing into the house, right? Wrong. You could

126

be dead wrong. We haven't covered safety equipment yet. I know some people think it's masculine to work without safety equipment, but I disagree strongly.

Salvage operations are dangerous. Just as you put on a coat to face nature's winter elements, you have to dress to face the elements of demolition. A demolition job site is a harsh environment.

Nails stick out everywhere; things can fall down; and, while force is being exerted on an object, it can suddenly break away and hit you in the face. It's as though you're inside a haunted house and it's out to get you. There is danger in every direction. Make sure you are prepared to face this danger—prepared like a soldier going into battle. Without proper preparation, you'll lose the war.

Once I was tearing lathing strips from the studs of a wall. I was prying from behind the strips, and they weren't coming loose. I exerted just a little more pressure, and snap! The lathing strips, nails and all, came flying at me before I could get my hands up to protect myself. They "exploded" from the wall, striking me in the face. Fortunately my eyes weren't injured because I was wearing *safety glasses.* I always wear them when tearing out materials. To do otherwise is an unacceptable gamble. You are gambling with your eyes.

I know safety glasses are often uncomfortable; the large plastic ones frequently fog up, and I don't like wearing them. I bought a pair of glasses for $10; they are comfortable, don't get in the way, and don't restrict or distort my vision. Since they are comfortable, I don't mind wearing them. Those big, bulky safety glasses do no good if they are not on your face. So, if you don't like wearing them, buy some safety lenses in ordinary frames.

Safety equipment includes, clockwise from left, face mask, leather gloves, two pairs of safety glasses and hearing protectors. And don't forget a hard hat.

When you dismantle a building properly, you reverse the building process.

Other safety items include *gloves*. Leather ones are preferred, although not absolutely necessary. Cloth will do.

You will need *boots* with thick soles. Leather soles work the best. Don't work in tennis shoes unless you like the feel of rusty steel going into your feet.

Also, pick up a cheap *hard hat*. If you don't like wearing a hard hat all the time, wear an ordinary knit beanie. A beanie is three times better than nothing. Wear *long pants* and a *long-sleeved shirt*; without them, you will pick up a few scratches. If it is too hot to wear these things, then it may be worth the risk of getting a few scratches.

If you will be tearing out old plaster walls, obtain a *face mask*. Some old plaster contains cancer-causing asbestos, and dust from it shouldn't be breathed into your lungs. Those little white masks that fit over your nose and mouth are virtually useless. Get a good mask. A good face mask traps particles in a replaceable filter.

One rarely used safety item is a pair of *earplugs*. When you're doing a lot of pounding or other noisy tasks, a set of earplugs will protect your ears. Americans lose their hearing at a much faster rate than do people of other countries; noise is the factor.

The safety equipment that is needed, then, is the following: safety glasses, gloves, thick-soled boots, long pants, a long-sleeved shirt, a face mask, earplugs, and a hard hat. You don't have to wear all this always, but it should be handy so you have it when you need it. Make a habit, though, of wearing your safety glasses all of the time.

It's Time to Begin

You've written your demolition contract, you've assembled your tools and safety equipment. You're ready to get started without risking life and limb for salvaged materials. Smart! You're ready to tear into that building on Easy Street.

Danger: Power

The very first item that must be investigated is whether there is electricity in the building. Most abandoned houses will have had the electrical power disconnected long ago; don't take a chance and assume this is true.

Test the electrical outlets by plugging in any electrical tool. Light sockets can be tested by screwing in a light bulb. Test all of the electrical outlets and light sockets to insure that the entire house is "dead."

If any of the lines are "hot," they can be disconnected at the circuit box. An electrician can easily do this work and can install a temporary outlet at the circuit box. Power tools can then be run off an extension cord plugged into this outlet.

If all outlets in the house are dead and the circuit box's main breaker is off, the circuit breakers can be shut off and the leads running through the house can be disconnected. Again, ask an electrician to do this work. Then the temporary hookup can be fashioned, and the main breaker can be turned on. Don't turn on the main breaker before disconnecting the leads, just in case the wires running through the house have been damaged by rodents or have deteriorated through time. Fires get started this way.

If there is no power at the house, ask the power company to hook up temporary service, a main line connecting the utility pole to the house. Often they will insist that a temporary outlet be installed and that all other lines running from the box be disconnected. They can then switch on the power.

Remote temporary outlets— outlets that are not connected to the house—are always possible, but are often too expensive to consider. It would be more economical to rent a gasoline-powered generator to run your saws.

The very important points to be made here are these:

1. Make sure that the lines running through the house are not live.
2. If you don't know much about electricity, have a qualified person modify the circuit box to provide you with a temporary outlet.

How to Start

When you dismantle a building properly, you reverse the construction process. If a movie were taken of the construction of the building and if that film were run backwards, you would see the precise order in which you would approach the job. Undoing a building is exciting because you learn its secrets, you learn how it is put together. You learn something about the people who put it together, too. A person can learn more about construction by dismantling a building than by probably any other means.

Removing the Trim

If you want to salvage every bit of available material, start with the doors and trim. If the house has interior doors, remove them first. Then insert a larger flat bar and loosen the trim. Don't try to get part of the trim free and then pull the piece away from the door jamb; instead, pry the entire piece away from the wall and jamb evenly. By removing it this way, the chances of breaking brittle trim are lessened.

Often wood molding is nailed from one piece into the other through the miter joint. This is the most likely place for the molding to break. See the angle at which the nails were driven. Then pull from the same direction and the trim should come free without breaking.

When using pry bars on trim that you expect to reuse, think about the best points to make contact with your tools. For example, the casing above the door should be pried away at the top since slight damage there will not be noticeable. Slight damage will occur as you remove the trim; just make sure the damage is in hard-to-notice places.

Label All Parts

Label the doors, jambs, and casing so that you can put them back together again exactly as originally installed. Do this by writing with a felt tip marker on masking tape applied to the pieces. Or if the trim will be painted, a spray-paint can makes for quick marking.

Sometimes you can remove the entire door, jamb, and casing at once. To do this, use the reciprocating saw to make cuts outside the casing all the way around the door. Then tip the entire unit out of its place. Complete door units are only reusable when they are placed in a wall with a thickness nearly identical to the wall thickness of the original building.

Here's the best way to free the jamb from the studs: insert bolt cutters or the reciprocating saw blade behind the jamb and cut the nails securing the jamb to the wall. If this can't be done, use a nail puller. Nail pullers will dent the jamb, but this is not a serious problem. The dents can be spackled and the entire jamb

LIGHTING AND ELECTRICAL

The lighting fixtures in a house may be of an interesting design and may be in good enough shape to salvage. If the wiring looks worn or brittle, an old fixture can be easily rewired with new wiring. The fixtures, though, are the only items that should be salvaged from the electrical system.

New wire is cheap. New wire should always be installed in new structures. Old wire is often damaged as it is removed—even if great care is taken. Where the wire was stapled to the wood framework of a house is where wire can easily be damaged—either when the wire was installed or when it is being removed. It is not worth the risk to use old wire. And, it is not worth the time it takes to carefully remove the old wire. Scrap it.

Old power outlets (duplexes) should not be reused. All codes require grounding outlets to be installed in new buildings. Grounding outlets can take a three-pronged plug. The old outlets can take only a two-pronged plug, and so are not valuable in any way. Besides, new outlets cost much less than one dollar.

FLOOR COVERINGS

Old carpeting and carpet padding are often reusable. Perhaps the carpeting does not look very good at all—it can then be used as padding for the new carpet you will buy as a finish floor covering. Old carpet makes fine padding, as does old padding. Padding does not have to be brand new to work well.

A carpet salesman would cringe at this notion, but this is a fine way to carpet: lay down some old padding that is still in pretty good condition, then lay down some old carpet. Next, the final layer of new carpet can be laid over these previous two layers. Especially for a slab floor, this is a good technique since it gives you an extra layer between your feet and the hard concrete.

The other benefit of that method is this: you can lay down the first two layers while the house is still in its completion stages. Then, after everything else is done, the final layer can be applied—giving you carpeting to live with as you finish your house and a brand new layer upon completion of your dwelling.

painted. Most salvaged trim requires painting after installation.

Now you're ready to tackle the remainder of the trim. When removing floor, window, and ceiling trim, use the same techniques you followed for the doors.

Kitchen Cabinets and Fixtures

The kitchen counter top and the cupboards are next. Usually, countertops are screwed to the cupboards beneath from inside the cupboards, so look inside for these screws. The cupboards are screwed to the wall from inside, too, so reach inside these cupboards and see what you can do. If you don't want the cupboards, it's time to try out the power bar. Jam it between the wall and the cupboards and let fly. The cupboard doors might be salvageable, and they might look fine painted, so give them a second glance before discarding them.

Look at the kitchen sink and other plumbing fixtures and determine what you will want. Heavy cast iron can be sold as scrap. So, even if you don't want to use these fixtures, consider selling them. In any case, get them out of the house so they are out of the way and don't crash through the floor when you're dismantling the framing.

The Finish Flooring

If you want the finish flooring, now is the time to remove it. Some old houses have nice oak flooring, and it may be in good shape. It is a little hard to salvage, but it can be done. You just have to wreck the first two

pieces next to the wall so you can get underneath the adjacent pieces. Pry these near where they are nailed, then remove the nails. Work very carefully since splintered flooring is worthless. When removing flooring, work from the tongue side of the board, just as the installer did.

At this point, look around and see if there is anything else you want to salvage that will be ruined if it is exposed to inclement weather. And see if there is anything you might want to tear out while protected by the shelter of the house, such as the fireplace mantle or brick. If there are any such things, remove them, because the next step is tearing off the roof.

Removing Bricks

If you would like to remove the brickwork on the fireplace, begin working from the top. Brickwork is removed by prying it away from the wall. A large crowbar is inserted behind the brickwork near the very top of the wall. Then the bar is pried repeatedly until the brickwork begins to loosen.

The area in front of the brick veneer wall should be clear of all tools, materials, and people. The bricks will not pry away one by one. Entire portions of the veneer wall will loosen, fastened together in one piece by the mortar. By starting near the top of the wall, smaller portions of the wall will become loose. Once loosened, the pieces can be dislodged with the hands and removed from the wall. It is important not to drop large portions of the wall onto the floor of the house since the impact could cause a weak floor to collapse.

Used bricks are worth saving. The mortar can be chipped off them with a hammer and chisel.

The Roof

Remove the shingles with a heavy-duty coal shovel. They're usually not worth saving. Working from the ridge, insert the shovel under the shingles and pry the shingles up. Be careful when working near the eaves. If the roof is too steep to stand on comfortably, nail 2×4s onto the roof by the eave so that in case you slip, there is a place to catch on to. It is best if two 2×4s are nailed atop each other to give at least three inches of wood to catch with the feet. When working on extremely steep roofs, tie one end of a rope around your waist, swing the other over the roof, and have it tied to the interior framing. Tie it to the chimney if that is very solid. Don't try to work too fast on a roof. Try only to be safe.

Once the shingles are removed, take off the roof sheathing, which can be saved. The nail puller comes in handy here. For the neatest job, pull each nail be-

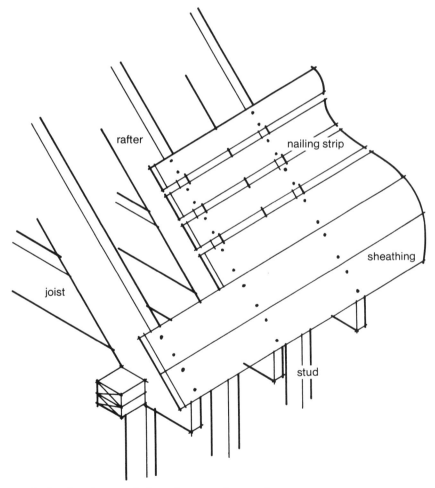

rafter
nailing strip
joist
sheathing
stud

Both the sheathing and the rafters can be saved.

HEATING EQUIPMENT

Old furnaces are bulky and inefficient. Generally, an old furnace is not worth saving. Since they are subjected to intense heat, they burn out after so many years.

The ductwork in a house less than twenty years old may be usable. New ductwork is not very expensive, though, so unless the old ductwork is easily removed and is in good shape, it is better to scrap it along with the furnace and begin with a brand new heating system to serve your heating purposes.

ROOFING MATERIALS

Roofing is not usually salvaged since it cannot be removed without damaging it. Wooden, asphalt, asbestos, and generally metal roofing all should be considered useless once removed.

The only materials worth salvaging are the hard roofing materials—slate and tile. These very expensive roofing materials can be salvaged without doing damage to them. And, once salvaged, they are very valuable.

Tile roofs are often interlocking and so are easy to remove. Slate roofs are nailed in place. Each piece of slate was pre-drilled in two places near the top. Then, it was nailed in place. By working carefully, slate roofs can be removed in good condition. Once reinstalled, a slate roof is permanent and is the most beautiful roof that a person can have. Remember, though, a slate roof must have a very steep pitch to keep from leaking.

131

fore prying up the board. If the boards have lap joints, work on two adjacent boards at one time.

Frequently it is easier to start at the top of the roof and work down. This way you can kneel on the roof while pulling nails. Tie boards in small bundles and use a rope to lower them to the ground. This is the safest way and insures that they won't crack when they hit the ground. If it is a single-story roof, the roof sheathing can often be dropped to the ground. Make it a practice to yell before throwing the boards down. You never know—

a neighbor may be walking around to see what is going on.

Brace the Rafters

The rafters may need temporary bracing before all of the roof sheathing boards are removed. If they're shaky, install braces either on the underside or on the top of the rafters wherever needed. Sometimes wire stapled onto the rafters to tie them together is sufficient bracing. If wire is sufficient, use it because it will facilitate the removal of the rafters, as I'll explain in just a minute.

Once all the sheathing has been removed, take down the rafters. They can be pried loose from the top plate of the wall or they can be cut loose. Either way is fine. Usually once a rafter is freed from the plate, it can be wiggled loose from the ridge board. If the rafters have collar ties, remove the collar ties first. Wire bracing facilitates rafter removal this way: when a rafter is wiggled loose from the ridge board, the wire supports the loose rafter temporarily; then it can be freed of the wire and taken down completely.

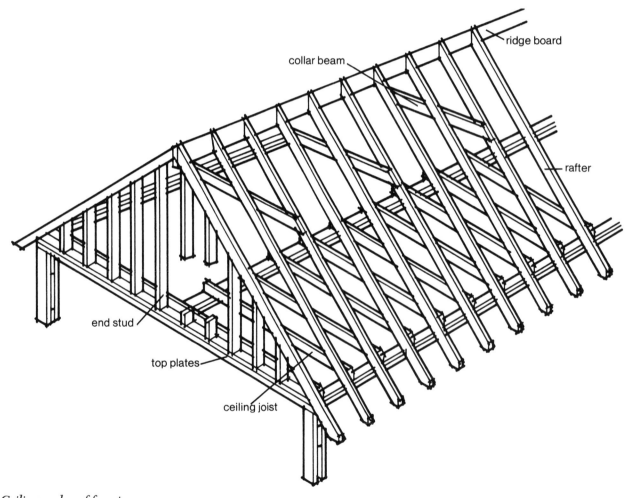

Ceiling and roof framing.

If, as is customary, there are ceiling joists below the rafters, you can lay pieces of plywood over the joists so they can be walked on easily. This facilitates the removal of the rafters. Once all the rafters are down, you can use the plywood for the next step.

The Ceiling Joists

Before the ceiling joists can be taken down, you must remove ceiling lathing and plaster. This is best done from atop the ceiling joists so the material won't fall on your head.

While keeping your balance, gently drop the sledgehammer against the lathing material at points where it is attached to the joists. After you do this down the line, the lathing will loosen and start to fall. No one should be below.

With the plaster down, you can remove the ceiling joists. They can be pried from the top plate of the wall which they rest on or they can be cut away. Usually it is easy to pry them loose with a crowbar. Sometimes, though, the old wood is quite brittle, making it more feasible to cut it away from its fasteners to salvage it in good condition. When the joists are down on the floor, clean off the remaining lathing material, then take them outside. And, to make your next step easier, spend some time cleaning up the inside of the house.

Now for the Walls

Now you have a house without a roof and without ceiling joists.

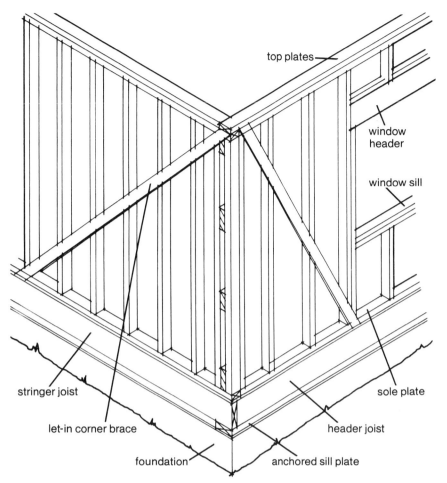

When you've removed the plaster and lath, you'll find something like this.

You have four exterior walls and some interior partitions. Remove the plaster and lath (or the drywall if the house is relatively new) from the interior partitions first. This is done by any means possible. It's impossible to salvage this material.

Sometimes it is easy enough to put on a pair of gloves and use a 4×4 like a battering ram—jamming it through the wall. Or, it may be more fun to get the crowbars out to pry the lathing away from the studs. Try to stay away from the direction of energy. Once one side of the partition wall material has been re-

moved, the opposite side is best attacked from the rear, forcing the material in the direction away from your body for safety reasons.

If after taking the lathing off the interior partition wall studs, you still have the energy and ambition to go after some more, proceed with the lathing on the exterior walls. This, too, must come off the studs. It is easier to pull the nails holding the lathing while the studs are still standing, so this is another job that can be worked on.

Switch off between jobs so your body has a chance to use

PLUMBING

Most old houses will have had their water turned off long ago. Main valves located at the water meter can be turned on, though, just to make sure that the water company has turned off the flow before it reaches the house. If they have not, inform them that it can be turned off so that you won't have to worry about faulty valves allowing some water to pass through the pipes as the pipes are being removed from the walls. Old valves often do not entirely stop the flow of water—just as old faucets will often leak.

With the water system shut off, the old pipes can be removed from the walls. Old homes usually have galvanized steel pipes, which are not generally reused. The deposits inside the pipes impede the flow of water; and, galvanized pipes are more difficult for most people to work with than are new copper pipes. It is better to work with new pipes, although if there are copper pipes in good condition, they can be used again. Or they can be cashed in as scrap metal. Copper is valuable.

The old-fashioned cast iron hub-type pipes can be reused for a new home's sanitary (waste) system. I've cut off the hub part of the pipe, and then used the pipes along with "no-hub bands," which is the modern way of attaching pipes. No-hub bands attach one pipe to another easily. The hub pipes were originally put together with leaded joints—a method of installation which would prove difficult to most plumbers today.

different muscles. Instead of weakening your shoulder muscles by overusing the battering ram, and then not having enough energy to pull the nails from the studs, batter down some lathing, pull a few nails, and when you get bored, get out the sledgehammer. It's almost time to knock out some of those studs.

Typically, partition walls are nailed to other walls, so the end stud on each side of the stud wall must be pried free of the grasps of the adjacent walls. Once this is done, the wall can be tipped over, and the wall's bottom plate can be freed from the studs. Generally, it will be quite loose by the time the wall is laid prone and sometimes the studs will come off without your help.

Next, remove the wall top plate with the sledgehammer. Now all of the studs are free, are in one piece, and are free of nails. Take them outside. You'll put them to good use when you start building.

Once all the partition walls are knocked down, disassembled, and removed, and once the exterior wall lathing is down, it is time to clean up. Get the coal shovel you used for the shingles, put on your face mask, and start shoveling the old lathing away from the house and start a bonfire. The plaster adds lime to the soil, so don't worry about that.

Remove the Windows

Before you tackle the exterior walls, you must remove the windows, even if you don't want to salvage them. You don't want broken glass all over the place. Glass takes a million years to decompose. Do someone a favor and don't spread it around. Eventually, it will cut someone.

Work from the inside. After removing the casing, you can take out the piece of wood that the sash rests against. Then the window will come right out.

Next, the Exterior Walls

Now it is time to attack the exterior walls. By looking at the corners of the exterior walls from the inside, you can see which walls were set up last. These walls should come down first. If it doesn't look as if it's going to be easy, make a saw cut down both corners of one wall just inside the first studs. That will free it up.

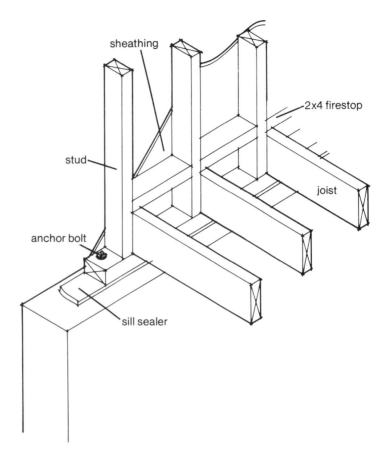

All of materials in the sill area can be salvaged.

BRICK VENEER HOMES

Homes with brick veneer must have the brickwork removed before the wall studs are removed. Beginning at the top of the wall, the brick can be pried at from behind to loosen portions of the brick wall. Once loose, the entire portion can be dropped to the ground.

If you are working from a ladder, it is important not to have any portions of the brick wall in front of your ladder, since that portion could tumble with the rest of the wall. Keep away from the direction of the fall. And, keep the area clear where the

bricks may fall. Oftentimes large portions of the wall will let go at once, giving you very little time to react.

If you have a situation where the first story of a house is bricked with the rest of the house being sided with a wood or other lightweight siding, it is best to wait to remove the brickwork until the second story of the house is torn down. Then you will be able to work from the second story floor *above* the brickwork, prying it away from the wall with your power bar.

135

Attach a rope to the top plate of the wall so it can be controlled as you drop it inside the house. Then, with the wall cut free, pull the rope and the wall should flop down with a loud bang.

Be careful: if the floor does not seem very strong, don't stand on it when the wall flops down. In this case, as before, tie the rope

---

STAIRS

Staircases rarely can be salvaged all in one unit since older homes typically have higher ceilings and thicker floors than the houses we are building today. To reuse a staircase all in one piece, you would have to build your home with exactly the same distance between floors. Although it is conceivable that one riser of the staircase could be eliminated, cutting down the height needed between the floors by about eight inches, generally one would not want to design a structure around a single staircase.

The valuable portions of a staircase are the treads—the part you step on. These treads can sometimes be loosened from the stairway stringers (the structure which the treads and the risers are attached to). With the treads freed, the rest of the staircase will probably be useless.

The exception to all of the above is a very beautiful staircase. In this case, it may be worthwhile to salvage it all in one piece and to design a new structure around it.

---

high on the wall. Then, from through the house and outside, pull the wall down.

With the wall down on the floor, you can remove the exterior siding, which often can be salvaged. The last piece of siding that was applied to the wall is at the top, so this is the first piece to remove. Work down the wall removing a piece of siding at a time. Remove the studs, using the same steps followed for the partition walls.

The other three walls are disassembled similarly. You may have to brace the walls once the first one is removed, to avoid an unexpected collapse. To do this, nail a 2×4 diagonally between the two top plates of adjacent walls. For long walls, attach a 2×4 high up on one of the wall

---

studs and nail it to a block nailed to the floor.

Once all of the exterior walls are dismantled, it is clean-up time again. All that is left is the floor platform, so it can be shoveled and swept clean. You don't have to get carried away with this. A large push broom can move a large amount of material in a quick and efficient manner.

The Platform

Generally, the platform is a source of two valuable materials: the floor joists and underlayment, which is boards, or in more recent buildings, plywood. Naturally, the underlayment comes up first. Extract the nails with the nail puller. Then pull up the underlayment boards evenly. I

SEWAGE

Removing a sanitary (or waste) system is not difficult. This is the system which has transported the sewage from the house to the city's sewage treatment plant. In the country, the systems lead to an owner's septic tank and drainage field. One need not fear about back-up since everything is tilted downhill. The insides of the pipes should be regarded as unclean. Undoubtedly, there are coliform bacteria still living inside; a certain amount of caution should be exerted.

The cast iron pipes can be cut apart with a carbide-coated blade attached to a circular saw. The

pipe can either be entirely cut through, or it can be scored with the blade and then severed with a hammer and cold chisel. Don't try to use a hacksaw blade on cast iron pipe, as it just won't work. Cast iron is hard stuff.

When cutting apart cast iron hubbed pipe, make the cut behind the hub on the pipe. The cut should be made evenly—then no further cutting is needed and the pipe can be joined together with a no-hub band to another pipe when the pipe is being reused.

One final note is this: cap the end of the pipe that leads to the disposal system to curtail odors.

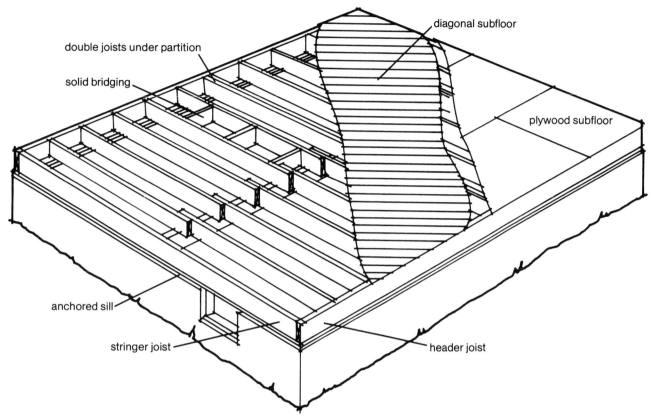

Here are the layers you'll find when removing the flooring.

In the diagram:
- double joists under partition
- solid bridging
- diagonal subfloor
- plywood subfloor
- anchored sill
- stringer joist
- header joist

have found that it is a mistake to leave loose boards on the floor. We are so accustomed to walking around on floors, we don't think about it, and so we'll walk over loose boards, sometimes not realizing it until it is too late and there's an accident. For this reason, pull up and remove the boards once they are loosened.

Floor Joists

With this done, the valuable floor joists remain. Be careful when removing the floor joists, since each one is worth at least $10. Pry them apart gently. With the floor joists removed, only the sills and basement girder remain. Usually, these are pried up easily. The girder may be a bit

INSULATION

Insulation may be salvaged if the house was insulated with batts of insulation at least 3½ inches thick. Lesser thicknesses of batt insulation are not really worth the effort it would take to salvage them. Many old homes have either no insulation or are insulated with 1½-inch batts faced with black paper. It is best to discard this as its insulating value is low, it is bulky to transport and store, and it is uncomfortable to work with. Most people find it to be quite irritating to the skin, and the fibers should not be inhaled.

When a house being razed contains 3½-inch or thicker batts, they may be successfully salvaged—as long as they are in good condition. Wet insulation is useless. If the batts are stapled to the studs, they may be removed quickly without the worry of ripping the paper moisture barrier. A new moisture barrier may be installed over the entire new wall after the insulation has been installed in its new location. Double moisture barriers are fine as long as one has been ripped or slashed substantially.

A long-sleeved shirt, gloves, and a face mask are helpful items when working with insulation. After removing the material, it should be rolled tightly and tied with string for efficient storage. Batts of insulation are rolled in the same way as one rolls up a sleeping bag.

heavy, though, so be careful where you stand in relation to where the girder could fall. The sills may be secured to the foundation with anchor bolts, so the nuts have to be removed before the sills can be lifted.

Two-Story House

If the house has two stories, you will have to repeat the process of taking down interior walls and exterior walls for the lower story. Everything's basically the same, though; it's just more work, time, and materials. Work from the top down, so you don't rip out load-bearing walls while they still support a load above.

Storing Your Materials

At this point, you have some neat piles of newly salvaged lumber, plus other materials, such as windows and doors. You also should have a neat little pile of ashes left over from burning the lath and the broken boards. Yes, there will be broken boards—probably a lot of them. Everything will not come off cleanly. If this stuff can be burned, great. If not, it will have to be hauled away. Some of it might be good firewood.

Your next steps will depend on your arrangements with the contractor with the dump truck and backhoe. If you have materials to be hauled away, pile them in one general vicinity. Make material piles neat so that they don't get confused with the trash. Once the rubbish is hauled away, it will be time to fill the basement with sand. First call the inspector, if this is part of your agreement, so he can see the basement is not full of organic material.

With this done, the basement can be filled in with sand and your job is complete. You've got your materials piled all over the place, and the next step is to transport them as quickly as possible to a safe storage area.

Wood should be stored up off the ground, and, if stored outside, it should be covered with plastic to keep it dry. Remove all nails and stack the wood evenly to keep it straight.

Like pieces of wood should all be stacked together. All of the ceiling joists that you have salvaged should be in one pile; the studs should be in another, and so on. When you use the lumber, you won't have to sort through the piles to find exactly what you need.

This preliminary work may seem a little excessive; yet the time spent making sure that your wood is properly stored will insure that it will remain straight and usable. Moreover, you will be able to find what you need when you want it.

PILE UP WOOD

A log-end home—inexpensive and practical

Earthwood is a two-story, circular house, built of cordwood masonry and sheltered by deep earth berms. Its core is twenty-five tons of masonry, a two-story stove that stores heat, then pours it out, long after the fire is out.

After more than a year in this house, I like it—its appearance, its ability to store heat, its layout, and its many comforts.

My wife, Jaki, and I built it with a minimum of outside help, hired to speed the construction. It's a home that could be built by many who are not skilled builders. Prior to constructing Earthwood in West Chazy, N.Y., Jaki and I had built two houses. Log End Cottage features cordwood masonry, the building style in which very short logs—called log ends—are laid widthwise in the wall like a rank of firewood. Log End Cave uses techniques conducive to low-cost underground construction.

Combining Techniques

At Earthwood, our goal was to combine these building techniques, and to add a new dimension to our experiments in low-cost house construction, which is to provide for all of the living systems—food production and preservation, energy conservation, recreation, and home industry—not just shelter.

By Robert L. Roy

Robert and Jaki at entrance to Earthwood

Our first plan for Earthwood called for a single-story 38'8" diameter round house with sixteen-inch thick cordwood walls supporting an earth roof. The evolution of the plan to a two-story building of the same diameter and wall thickness was, strangely enough, a function of economics.

As we got close to our spring, 1981, start, I estimated that the materials' cost of the original 1,000-square-foot design would be about $12,000, or $12 per square foot. Two of the more ex-

139

pensive components of the house structure would be the foundation and the roof. I wondered what it would cost to sandwich another cordwood story between this expensive foundation and the expensive roof. We would need an extra five cords of wood for log ends, the additional mortar, a few extra posts, floor joists, 1,000 square feet of planking, stairs, some internal framing, and a few more doors and windows. The driveway, windplant, and water and septic systems would be, like the roof and foundation,

common to the building, whether it be 1,000 square feet or 2,000. I figured the materials' cost of the second story to be about $4,000, or $4 per square foot—too cheap to turn down.

I had discovered the economy of two-story construction, which had already been discovered by millions of people before me, of course. Heating the two stories also made sense, especially if a radiant heat source—a masonry stove, in our case—was located at the center of the lower story. No point on the inner surface of

the cordwood wall would be more than sixteen feet from the thermal mass. The huge cylindrical masonry stove would operate at a higher temperature near the bottom, heating the downstairs first. Then the warm air would rise through the open circular staircase to the second story, the main living area. Voila! The heat is used twice before it leaves the house.

The Extra Space

It didn't take me long to figure out what to do with the extra space: 250 square feet for a pool table (recreation), 150 square feet for son Rohan's play area (kids need recreation, too), 125 square feet for my office (home industry), 80 square feet for a root cellar and battery storage area for a future wind-electric system (food preservation and energy). It was easy to justify a big house by labeling the spaces to show how they corresponded to an integrated living system, although the cordwood hot tub was tough to label. Thus, Earthwood evolved as a charming blend of wisdom, folly, and excuses.

At about the time that the house plans doubled in size, the idea of earth-sheltering the walls was growing stronger and stronger. I'd often been asked at workshops if cordwood could be used below grade, and, if so, how. I had replied that, yes, it could be, but only with a curved wall, as cordwood has very little tensile strength with which to resist lateral pressure.

François Tanguay of Quebec

Structural plan of the Round House.

Laying out a round house is easy; nothing has to be squared. All measurements and grade readings for the setting of the footing forms is done from the center point. We used Dow Styrofoam beneath the footings to stop the "energy nosebleed" which often occurs at this point in earth-sheltered houses.

had used cedar log ends in his circular basement wall, which had simply been tarred prior to backfilling. The success of his basement, I think, comes from proper backfilling with good coarse sand, allowing water to percolate easily to the four-inch perforated tile drain below.

It was my intent to try a waterproofing method of greater durability, as our lower story was meant to function as an important living area, not simply a wood store, as at the Tanguay house. More about this waterproofing technique later.

Most people now know that the advantage of earth-sheltering a home is *not* that earth is a great insulator—it isn't—but that it stores heat and is slow to change temperature. Building an earth-sheltered home in northern New York has the effect of moving construction 800 miles or so south, to—say—North Carolina. But, while 40° F. is a lot better starting temperature than −20°, it is still cold. Insulation is needed to prevent dissipation of the internal heat to the planet. We will not succeed in significantly warming the earth with our homes. However, we can use the massive building structure it-

self for heat storage, our own more reasonably scaled "thermal flywheel." The key is the proper placement of a bio-nondegradable insulation, such as Dow Styrofoam, on the exterior of the structure.

Chose Hardwood

We decided on dense hardwood log ends below grade, because of their greater thermal mass than softwoods. My experience with cordwood masonry up to this time had been limited to the use of northern white cedar, excellent for above-grade applications because of its high insulative value. And the most common problem reported with cordwood construction has been that of wood shrinkage, the result of using wood which had not been seasoned long enough. It did not occur to me that there could be another—potentially more serious—problem with using very dry hardwood: cordwood expansion. Listen to this:

The Earthwood building is built on a slab. About 40 percent of the wall area is bermed, mostly on the northern hemisphere. We decided to use cedar log ends for the portion of the house exposed above grade, because of the insulation advantage. We began to build, carefully covering the walls each night so that rain would not get into the cavity between the inner and outer mortar joints. (We insulate this cavity with dry sawdust to which lime has been added to protect against insect infestation, 1½ shovels of lime per wheelbarrow of sawdust.)

Water Swelled Wood

Even though we'd protected the wall from rainwater from above, we had not anticipated any problem with the water which collected on the slab and eventually made its way upward by capillary action to the first course of cordwood. The wood fibers of the dense hardwood—dry as old baseball bats—swelled with the rainwater, and with enough force to put pressure on the mortar joints. The wall took the line of least resistance,

which—because the wall was round—was to tilt outwards. At six feet of height, the wall was three inches out of plumb. We had to pull the wall down, using a pickaxe to jimmy the log ends out of the mortar.

Tried Again

Groan. We tried again with a different mortar mix, thinking that our usual sawdust mortar, designed to slow the curing process and eliminate mortar shrink-

age, had caused the cordwood wall to remain plastic too long, resulting in an outward pressure as we built around the circle. Nice guess ... but wrong. We consulted other cordwood builders and even an engineer, who suggested expansion joints, which we tried. One of the cordwood builders who had experienced a similar problem suggested pre-swelling the log ends in a bucket of water prior to laying up. We tried all these things, but our efforts were too little, too

The first course of concrete blocks is laid in mortar to establish level. A ⅝″ gap is created on the exterior because of the large circumference of the wall. This gap and the key slot, which comes as a part of 8″ corner blocks from our local block plant, are filled with mortar prior to surface bonding. No mortar is used between courses.

Cordwood masonry is fun and easy . . . but time-consuming. A double bed of mortar is laid, with the cavity between filled with sawdust. The log-end is placed with a slight vibrating motion to assure a good bond.

cedar was able to act as its own expansion joint; the wood fibers could swell into the air voids of the log end itself, without putting an outward pressure on the mortar matrix.

This new understanding did little to help us at the Earthwood building, however, as we had not laid by enough cedar to replace the overdry hardwood. So we fell back on another method of wall construction which we'd tried and proven at Log End Cave: the surface bonding of dry-stacked concrete blocks.

This simple technique of applying a tensile membrane of cement and fiberglass to both sides of a block wall is easy for the first-time owner-builder to learn, as well as being extremely quick and incredibly strong compared with the conventional style of laying blocks with mortar. We use a product called Foundation Coat (made by Conproco, Box 368, Hooksett, NH 03106) because of its manufacture with Type AR (alkali-resistant) glass fibers, the only kind approved for use by the tough Massachusetts building codes, incidentally.

Chose Big Blocks

As we wished to build a sixteen-inch cordwood wall on top of the blocks which we were now forced to use below grade, we chose 8×8×16 corner blocks for the job, and laid the wall like stacked cordwood. The wall, of course, was curved, resulting in a ⅝-inch gap between blocks on the exterior. These had to be filled with mortar prior to the application of the surface bonding cement. We filled the block

late. The wall came down a second time.

The cedar wall in the southern part of the house was causing us no trouble in the meantime, and it, too, was popcorn dry. I was beginning to get a sense of what was happening. A friend's story of how 19th century stone quarriers had broken off new faces of stone had helped me to see the light. The old timers had drilled holes in the stone, jammed the

holes with tight-fitting dowels of dry hardwood, watered the wood, and stepped back to watch the swelling dowels break off a foot and a half of granite.

A Costly Error

The problem with the overly dry hardwood had cost us six weeks and $2,000 worth of labor, materials, and aspirin. I finally concluded that the light and airy

A finished cordwood wall. The large stones retain the earth berm.

which tends to absorb light. Finally, the block wall stores heat better than the heaviest wooden wall.

Waterproofing Wooden Wall

I must report, for the benefit of others so inclined, that we did experiment with the application of a quality membrane to the hardwood wall prior to its dismantling. By working to a curved form, we had been able to keep the outer circumference of the cordwood wall quite regular. The rough log ends proved to be an excellent receiving surface for a parging mix of three parts sand, one part masonry cement. We scratched the first coat while still wet, using the point of the trowel. A smooth second coat of the same mix was applied to the "scratch coat," creating a perfectly smooth outer wall surface. We found that the W. R. Grace Bituthene 3000 waterproofing membrane adhered beautifully to the smooth cylindrical walls. I consider this technique to be greatly superior to simply tarring the outer surface of the cordwood wall. Of course, good drainage characteristics in the backfilling material are still of paramount importance, in order to take the pressure off any waterproofing system, no matter how good it is.

More Hands at Work

The months of September and October were a race against time. Our assistant from the start, Dennis Lee, was promoted from laborer to full-time cordwood mason, and we hired a new

cores with sand for greater thermal mass.

The block wall saved our necks, and turned out to be a blessing in disguise. Production leaped forward. Laying up cordwood is much slower than putting up surface bonding blocks. Soon we'd made up most of the six weeks of time we had lost,

and, after a few weeks of serious doubt, it became apparent that we could indeed get the house closed in before the advent of the cruel North Country winter ... if we worked like crazy.

Moreover, the interior of the smooth curved white block wall has a much better light-reflecting quality than the cordwood,

man, Kork Smith, to mix mud and prepare log ends.

With Kork laboring, Dennis and I laying wood, and Jaki pointing the mortar matrix, work progressed steadily, despite some discouraging cold, wet weather.

Masonry Stove

The masonry stove, built by Steve Englehart, a local mason experienced in the art, progressed on weekends, at about the same rate as the walls. Dennis and I supplied the labor for the project. (Sometimes Earthwood was a seven-day-per-week job; sometimes a day or two of rain would give us time off, wanted or unwanted.)

The masonry stove reduces from a five-foot diameter cylinder to four feet at its first floor height. The six-inch shelf thus created supports the radial floor joist system. Because of the chimney in the masonry, using the stone cylinder for structural support as described is in violation of some strict state building codes, such as those of Connecticut and Massachusetts. However, the system is safe because of the relatively low temperatures generated in the twenty-five-ton masonry stove. A perceptive building inspector should grant a variance. Again, at the roof, the stove reduces to a three-foot diameter cylinder, and the heavy 5×10 and 6×10 rafters are supported by the massive stone column.

Spruce Decking

We decked both the first floor and the ceiling with seasoned 2×6 tongue-in-groove spruce, a pretty floor—and ceiling—when

The masonry stove is five feet in diameter through the first level, reducing to a four-foot diameter at the second story. The 6″ shelf thus created supports the floor joist system.

145

laid down using the radial rafter system. There was very little wastage of material, because we started our planking at the perimeter of the building and worked inward, always using smaller and smaller pieces.

The 4×8 hemlock floor joists and the heavy red pine rafters are exposed, their spans supported midway by a sturdy octagonal post-and-beam framework of large, carefully selected barn timbers. The house is designed to support a combined earth and snow load of 150 pounds per square foot, which allows an eight-inch earth roof in our part of the snow belt.

We used the W. R. Grace Bituthene 3000 waterproofing membrane on both the surface-bonded block walls and directly upon the dry spruce roof planking. We have not encountered a single leak in either the walls or roof since this membrane was installed in October, 1981. On the earth-bermed walls, we protected the membrane with two inches of Dow Styrofoam extruded polystyrene insulation. The proper placement of the insulation on the *exterior* of the wall protects the membrane from freeze-thaw cycling and enables the walls to be used effectively as thermal mass. Extruded polystyrene has been found to retain 95 percent of its starting R-factor of 5.4 per inch after twenty years, with the 5 percent deterioration occurring during the first few months.

Two Layers

On the roof, we used four inches of Styrofoam, the second two-inch layer covering the cracks of the first. A roof with only R22 of insulation may not seem impressive for a climate where R38 is the recommended minimum, but earth roof requirements are a bit different from conventional roofs. With the planking (R2) and the eight inches of earth with its hay layers and grass cover (R8), the value is probably more like R32.

The seldom appreciated advantage of a shallow earth roof is that it maintains the snow cover, which Charles Wing, writing in his *From the Ground Up* (Little,

The radial floor joist system is supported by the walls, an octagonal post-and-beam framework, and the masonry stove mass.

146

After priming the surface-bonded wall with the compatible primer supplied, we applied the W. R. Grace Bituthene water-proofing membrane vertically to the wall.

roof. Without green cover, it would just wash away come spring. We began to heat the mass of the masonry stove—gradually, to minimize expansion cracking—and were able to hold our annual Guy Fawkes Night bonfire party at Earthwood on November 6. (These bonfires, coming conveniently at the end of the building season, are a great opportunity to tidy up the work site . . . and a good excuse for a well-earned booze-up.)

Easy to Heat

As we were comfortable at Log End Cave, and there was still quite a bit of interior finish work at Earthwood, we slowed our harrowing pace of the past few months. By firing the masonry stove once or twice every other day, it was easy to maintain a temperature of 50°. We were—and remain—delighted with the performance of the stove. It is clear now that my preliminary estimates of Earthwood's heating requirements of four cords of wood per year will be close to the mark . . . and we live in an 8500 degree-day area. An Oval wood-burning cookstove provides winter cooking and hot water, while supplementing the masonry stove for space heating. It is good to have another heat source for "quick heat," which the masonry stove will not provide.

Benefits of Round House

We have found that there are a number of pleasant benefits to a round house which we had not expected. One is that the solar

Brown and Company, 1976), places at R1 per inch. This corresponds with our experience at Log End Cave, where we have observed that with the disappearance of the snow in late March, in combination with low earth temperatures, we burn almost as much firewood in March

and April as in the more severe winter months.

A big push enabled us to get the house closed in by November 1 . . . just in time. We covered the roof Styrofoam with a layer of hay and two inches of crushed stone for the winter. There was no point in placing earth on the

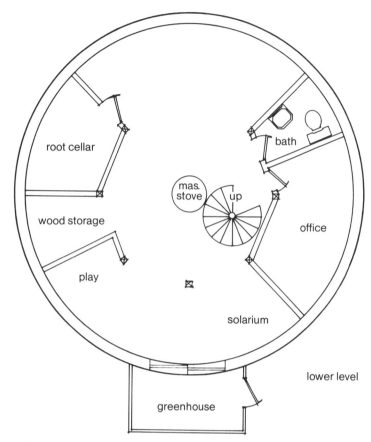

Floor plan for Earthwood.

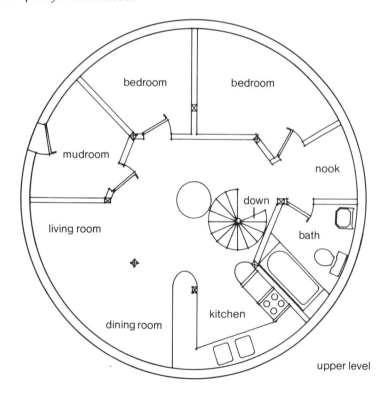

gain through the double-pane windows is much greater than anticipated, especially during the cold months of November through February, when the sun's arc is close to the horizon and the life-giving rays penetrate to the center stone mass. There are always three or four windows on each story with a nearly direct angle to the sun.

Another pleasant surprise at Earthwood is the congenial combination of shapes, curves, and angles, especially in the large open-plan room upstairs, but also in the bedrooms. The eye is carried around by the house curvature and is not frequently trapped in a corner. The radial rafter system, with the exposed planking above, draws the eyes to the center of the building, where they can take pleasure in Steve Englehart's fine stonework, truly the focal point of the house.

Hard to Build?

People ask if it is not a great deal more difficult to build a round house. It is not. In fact, with masonry walls, it is probably easier than building a rectilinear shape, as there are no right angles to worry about. All positions and measurements are taken radially from the fixed center point. Because a circle encloses the greatest area per perimeter foot, there is actually less work in building a round house than a square one of the same area. Birds and beavers, of course, have known this for years. This happy accident of geometry comes into play again when it comes time to heat the

This picture, taken about half way through the project, shows clearly the extent of the earth-bermed portion of the house. From here on up, cordwood takes over, all exposed above grade. About 40% of Earthwood's walls are earth sheltered, virtually all of this on the northern hemisphere.

building. The relationship between the skin area and the usable floor area is still one of the most important considerations in designing an energy-efficient home, even an earth-sheltered or super-insulated design.

The only slight problem with the curved wall is the obvious: furniture is not designed to fit against a curved wall. Actually, we have found that very little space at Earthwood is lost in this way, because of the rather large thirty-six-foot internal diameter. Even a seven-foot couch placed against the curved wall loses only about three inches of space

behind it at the midpoint.

Kitchen cabinet construction may have been the biggest problem created by the curved walls. This job probably took between a quarter and a third more time than if the kitchen had been square.

Looking Ahead

As mentioned at the outset, the intention with the Earthwood design was to attend to all the living systems simultaneously, not just shelter. I hope to report the final results on this in a book to appear in 1983. As of

this writing, I can say that the building performs excellently with regard to providing comfortable and pleasing shelter, energy-efficiency, and plenty of good quality space for food preservation, recreation, and home industry.

The greenhouse, garden, sauna, shed, and finished landscaping are all scheduled for our second season on the project. The intent is to build raised bed gardens (French intensive biodynamic gardening) on the south side of the main building, just in front of the greenhouse. Plants will be started in the greenhouse,

Earthwood in November, 1981, closed in for the winter.

which will also serve as an auxiliary heat source during the winter. Excess rainwater not required to maintain the green cover of the roof will be carried by gutters to two large oak barrels, reservoirs for a gravity siphon drip irrigation system. During dry spells, the barrels can be filled with an outdoor pump over our well, already in place.

Costs

The bottom line? Well, all the returns are not in yet, but I'll wager that the following breakdown is within 10 percent of the truth: Materials for the house, including plumbing and electric: $14,000. Heavy equipment contracting, including driveway, New York State–approved septic system, well, and preliminary landscaping: $3,000. Labor: $8,000. Total: about $25,000. The house has about 2,000 square feet usable—based on internal dimensions—so the cost per square foot is about $12.50. In addition, Jaki and I have about 3,000 hours in the main building, with more to come on the outbuildings, garden, and landscaping.

Cordwood masonry is labor-intensive, but the result is worth it. I would recommend the technique to anyone with wood as an indigenous resource, and more time than money. I would *not* recommend a building the size of Earthwood as a first-time project for the inexperienced owner-builder. Jaki and I had the dual advantages of previous building experience and a comfortable home to retreat to just a half-mile away. And we still found the project to be quite stressful, although the largest part of the stress came from the problem with the expanding hardwood.

My advice to a first-timer, interested in a similar kind of house, would be to build the single-story, twenty-foot diameter shed first. This would provide on-site, rent-free, living accommodation; building experience in the same techniques to be employed on the main building later, and, more important, an insight into what you're getting yourself involved with on the main building.

SCAVENGE

It's the way to save money and build a house with character.

Alan Roebuck Photos

Recycled materials were used throughout.

Scavenging materials to build a house is much harder than placing an order and having everything delivered. But, there are so many advantages that make it worthwhile.

The economic advantages are obvious—you'll save a bundle of money. Remember that having the materials delivered is easy—paying for them is the hard part. When you've finished scavenging, you won't be in debt for thirty years.

By scavenging materials, you'll also have a house that is truly yours. It will have links with the past, features that in future years will remind you of your experiences in finding them. Other people will enjoy your house too. A scavengered house never ends up bland, mundane, or characterless.

Finally, there's a joy to scavenging, finding materials for free that would cost hundreds at the building supplies store, locating just the right door or window, continuing the life of an-

tique fixtures in a new setting. I'll always remember finding the last items needed to complete matching sets—sets of doors, sets of knobs, sets of matching rafters. Finding the last piece is like completing a puzzle.

My house is full of recycled material. Some of it is obvious; much of it is hidden behind other finishing material. The materials that are left open to view are all matching and are all in good condition. A scavenger/builder must use discretion when determining which materials should be used in any given location.

When designing my house of the second-hand materials, I tried to keep one thought in mind: make it simple and small enough to be easily managed. The result is a one-story house with a shed-style roof and cathedral ceilings. The roof was easy to construct, and the high ceilings lend a feel of spaciousness inside.

Berming

The house is earth-bermed on all four sides, and has broad windows on the southwest side. These features keep heating costs low. High clerestory windows admit light and heat in the winter; an overhang shields them from the sun in the summer. These windows provide a good view from the inside. You can see the treetops and the sky, a much

By Alan D. Roebuck

better view than your neighbor's aluminum siding.

The earth berming used the excavated dirt left over from flattening the area where the house would stand. Instead of removing the dirt (and paying removal costs and dumping charges), the dirt was left on the site and scraped back against the foundation to make the berm.

The berming provides the needed frost protection for the footings. Here in Michigan, footings must be forty-two inches below finish grade to be protected against the dangers of frost heaving the ground. Instead of trenching forty-two inches below the floor level and then filling this trench up with concrete, I poured the footings at slab level and composed a forty-two-inch-high foundation wall. On the outside, the earth berm was piled up against this foundation wall. On the inside, I had achieved forty-two inches of finished wall.

Building Forms

Since this wall is composed of poured concrete, formwork had to be made to contain the concrete. The exterior form was made of half-inch plywood. The interior form was made from roof sheathing boards I had salvaged from an old house that was being torn down. These boards were peppered with nails. Instead of pulling out all these nails, I pounded them in—making them protrude into the cavity which would be filled with concrete.

After the concrete wall had

Before foundation was poured, earth was pushed away.

Then earth was pulled back, to form berm.

been poured and had set for three days, the exterior formwork was removed. The half-inch plywood was later used for wall sheathing. The interior formwork composed of the old sheathing boards was retained, now fulfilling a new purpose as the foundation wall's finish paneling. All of the nails, which were pounded in securely, fasten the paneling to the poured con-

Roof sheathing boards were used for interior of form.

crete wall. Once wire-brushed and thoroughly washed to remove concrete residue, I coated the paneling with linseed oil. This preserves it, darkens it, and brings out the patterns in the wood. It now has the look of barnwood siding.

Typically, a foundation wall will protrude a minimum of six inches out of the ground, providing moisture protection for the wooden portions of the house. I did not want bare concrete exposed beneath the wood siding, so I topped the concrete wall with six inches of stone imbedded in concrete. This provided a visual starting point for the house.

Pattern in Concrete

To compose this stonework, I salvaged some boards to make forms. The wood was severely charred—the result of a fire at the building long ago. The charring had left a pattern on the wood, with denser areas raised in relief from the softer areas which had burned away to a greater depth. This pattern was transferred to the concrete when it was poured and hardened, and was attractive.

This technique for making stonework can be done by anyone. Once the forms are made and are set in place, the hard concrete below is dampened to help bond it to the new concrete. The new concrete is shoveled into the formwork to a depth of about two inches. Then, large stones are embedded in the concrete. I placed the stones in the forms so that the flatter portion of the stone would rest against the formwork. This way more of the stone would show once the formwork was removed. With this first layer of stones in place, a layer of concrete is worked in between the stones until the stones are covered. Then another layer of stones is placed in the form, followed by another layer of concrete. This final layer of concrete is leveled off to the top of the formwork.

By stripping off the formwork after three hours, I could still work the concrete, although it had begun to set. Using a spoon, I scraped off concrete from the face of the stones to expose more of each stone.

When this band of stonework was completed and had cured for three days, I attached a wooden sill to the top of this "string course" of stone. Conventional wood frame construction followed for the portions of the walls above the stonework. Many salvaged 2×4s were incorporated into this wall framework (as well as the half-inch plywood which was used for the concrete foundation formwork). All of this wooden wall structure gets covered by finishing materials, so as long as you don't tell anyone what's inside my walls, no one will ever know!

Siding

I was a little bit in limbo about what to use for the finish exterior siding for my house—until I saw the "waste strips" that were delivered along with my roof beams. Yes, I have to admit that I bought my roof beams new. They were delivered to the site by a trucker who owed my father a favor. They were monsters— the largest thirty-six feet long and measuring four by fourteen

Midway in construction, with berm in place.

inches. My father had the mill yard throw on the strips which were cut from each surface of my beams. Every beam is shaven to bring it down to a proper dimension size and to expose the pink of the wood beneath the weathered exterior of the unmilled slab of wood.

Sawyers will cut strips off from the surfaces of the beams—these are the "waste strips"—which are as thick as an inch. I looked at them and thought about the exterior siding I needed for my house. Right there I had enough to do the front of the house. The next week I returned to the mill and picked up a large bundle of the "waste." It made fine siding.

I found other uses for the "waste strips," too. I used them for shelving, paneling for one of my rooms, and even facing for the exterior doors so they would match the exterior siding. And, by ripping the thinner pieces on a table saw, I used them for the interior trim.

Doors

The interior doors in my house are the old-fashioned panel style doors. I searched until I found all five-panel doors so that they would all match. I didn't try to make these doors look like new. Instead I patched some of the holes, scratches, and gouges; after sanding down the blistered paint and flaking varnish, I painted them black.

Two flea markets provided the hardware for the doors. The hinges weren't much cheaper than new hinges, but are of cast iron and have an attractive de-

tailed pattern. The porcelain knobs, which I found in Virginia, and the key plates complement the old doors. The beautiful results made the search for them— almost a scavenger hunt— worthwhile.

Two of the three interior doors lead to the bathroom, one from the master bedroom, the other from the living area. The floor of that bathroom is a link to the agricultural past of the nation. Years ago, the poorer farmers in this area had wooden silos, the average farmers had concrete silos, and the richest had ceramic silos. The ceramic silo was made up of foot-square ceramic tiles, glazed on both sides. These tiles were mortared together, then reinforced with steel strapping. It took forty-eight tiles to make the circumference of a silo about

154

fifteen feet in diameter. Each tile, then, has about a seven-degree bend in its surface, not enough to cause trouble for me.

I salvaged tiles from a blown-down ceramic silo. By mortaring pieces of these tiles together for the floor, I made a waterproof and easy-to-clean surface. I used other tiles for beneath a wood stove, where they make an attractive and fireproof surface.

Tiled Tub

The bathroom has other tile-work, too. The entire bathtub is composed of white ceramic tile over four-inch poured concrete insulated with four inches of rigid foam. Since it is walled in on three sides, the tub is entered by stepping down at one of the narrow ends, instead of the wide side, as is normal. The shower head is pointed to the rear of the tub. This means there's no need for a shower curtain, which is nice.

The silo tile hearth I made is for the wood stove in the rear bedroom. The hearth is made up of fifteen of these tiles, and, to form a square, the sixteenth space is made of solid concrete, fine as a base for splitting wood.

The stove itself is an old one, made in Kalamazoo, Michigan. I bought it in Ohio. Behind it is another find, a slab of Tennessee marble from the interior of a building that was being renovated. A friend helping with the renovation was asked to take the slab to the dump. He called me and asked if I'd like it. I took it from the site to a marble shop and had them cut it down to size so it would fit perfectly behind

the silo tile hearth. Now it is a beautiful decoration which stores heat from the stove.

The stove in the living room has a hearth which is made from slate my father had left over from a patio he had built. Then I made a stone wall for behind the stove using the same technique I had used for making the stone-

work atop the concrete foundation of my house. This stove is near the kitchen so that it can be used for both cooking and heating.

Kitchen Counter

In the kitchen is a wooden countertop which is of the

Counter top once was school door.

butcher block style. This countertop used to be a door. I helped to tear down a temporary school building that had been erected for an overflow of children. One of the doors had a core of solid pieces of wood laminated together, but then covered with two layers of plywood veneer.

A friend, Pete, was helping me build my house. Being a bit of a wild man, he attached three circular-saw blades to the circular saw to duplicate (in a crude manner) a rabbeting blade. He ran this back and forth across the door surfaces, removing only the two veneer layers. Then we smoothed the surface with the belt sander. I polyurethaned the surface, and the door now looks like a costly butcher block. The wood is too soft for cutting on, but serves well as a smooth, clean surface for preparing food.

Furniture

It wouldn't make much sense to build a low-cost house and then spend $10,000 on furniture. Often hand-built furniture goes well with a hand-built house. I built my couch and my bed, and I fabricated a simple drawing table.

The couch was built with 2×4s and some good-looking pine boards, which used to be false beams in a restaurant. I splurged a bit and used oak boards to trim the couch. They are stained golden oak and then polyurethaned for a durable finish. I bought pre-cut foam for the cushions, then sewed together covers for them.

The drafting table is exactly two feet wide and eight feet long. I cut a standard-size piece of particle board in half, then glued the pieces together, for greater strength. I covered it with plastic laminate. Two filing cabinets with plastic laminated particle board boxes on top (to match the table) provide the base for the tabletop.

I built a raised water bed in the rear master bedroom. It has storage space beneath it, for such things as Christmas tree ornaments, a camping tent, and a hundred other items. The frame and legs are made from beams which I salvaged from a barn built in the Civil War era. The barn had been razed, so the beams were deep in rubble. We jerked them out with a long chain attached to a pickup truck.

In building the bed, I used a chain saw to notch one beam into another. Then I bolted salvaged steel L iron sixteen inches on center under the beams. Three-quarter-inch plywood covers the steel and supports the mattress. Incidentally, the plywood is covered with floor tile. It used to be part of a stage.

Builder splurged on oak boards for couch.

Save on Carpeting

Carpeting for most homes is expensive. Mine wasn't. I bought it from a supply house that acquires carpeting after it has been used at a convention for three or four days. It takes a lot of abuse at a gathering such as that, with distinct traffic patterns showing through portions of it. But much of it looks brand new, and by buying and cutting the carpet selectively, pieces large enough to cover an entire room can be salvaged without any traffic patterns showing. I bought all the carpeting for my house for $40, and I'm happy with it.

Beneath the carpet, I placed padding of used carpet and used padding. Placing two layers for padding gives the concrete floor a soft feeling. Old carpet for this use can be obtained, usually free for the taking, from carpet installers.

Salvaging together a house is a very adventuresome task. By using this approach, I accomplished two things I wouldn't have otherwise been able to accomplish: I completed an entire house, and, I composed a home which is unique and very personal.

FIND A STATION, A SCHOOLHOUSE, OR A CHURCH

Sturdy buildings, they often can be converted to houses.

The changing tides of society offer housing opportunities for the alert.

Buildings, still structurally sound, gradually disintegrate when unused, unless someone recognizes new opportunities for their use.

Across the country this happens, particularly with public buildings that have outlived the need for which they were built.

Ray Bearse watched it happen in Vermont. The Rutland Railway halted its passenger trains, and no longer needed its chain of small stations that stretched the length of the state. Education shifted from the convenience of many one- and two-room schools to the greater educational opportunities of central schools and a fleet of buses. The attitude of Vermonters toward religion changed. Once a small town could support several churches, each with its own creed. Today one community church may serve the needs of most of the townspeople, and several buildings, high-ceilinged, steepled, and sturdy as forts, are left vacant. In the following pages, Ray Bearse chronicles, with words and photographs, those changes, and the opportunities they have provided Vermonters to find new homes.

A Depot, Moved in Pieces

West Sandgate, Vermont, is a half-dozen houses nestled about a crossroads high in the Taconic Mountains straddling the Vermont–New York border.

It's odd to find high on a mountainside a former railroad depot miles from any past or present trackage. It's even odder when you see the depot sign. McIndoes. That former whistle-stop, in northeastern Vermont along the Connecticut River, is nearly 150 miles from Sandgate.

Daniel Settani, whose home is in East Bethel, Connecticut, moved the station to West Sandgate, and still owns it.

He bought it in 1968. "Paid $500 for it. We broke it down into about seven or eight sections. We made that many round trips from McIndoes to West Sandgate. That's about 2,500 miles.

"I worked on it over a period of years. Did my own work. I'm a building contractor. First, we dug out a semicellar. We then re-erected sections one by one and fitted them together. It's worked out pretty well.

"Once it was all together, I took a look at those fifteen-foot

high ceilings. I put in a second floor which now has four bedrooms and two baths. Cut windows into the upstairs walls.

"On the first floor I made the big waiting room into a large, comfortable living room. The former ticket office is now a bar. Kitchen and spare rooms are in the basement. We built a sun deck around three sides of the first floor."

Buy—and Move— a Depot

Most people who buy railroad stations for homes move them— and for a very practical reason. If there's still traffic on the line, they don't want trains rumbling past quite that close to their homes.

Walter and Hazel Davis did this when they bought the East Wallingford station. He moved it several hundred yards away from the tracks to a spot with a beautiful river view. Now the front of the building, with the small telegrapher's position jutting out from it, faces the river, and the almost windowless rear faces Route 103.

The Davises found the station provided them with a lot of room—room enough for a large

Ray Bearse Photos

The former McIndoes station is now a home in West Sandgate, Vermont.

Davis home was moved away from the railroad tracks.

living room with fireplace, a kitchen, bath, bedroom, and den downstairs, and another bedroom, bath, and storage upstairs. Davis did all of the conversion.

Readin', Ritin', and Renovations

The American flag still flies daily over the Hammondsville School, but there's been many another change to the little, red schoolhouse where so many youngsters learned their three Rs.

Gone are the blackboard that covered one wall, the school

Abandoned railroad stations like this one can still be found along unused railroad lines throughout the country.

Earl home once was a schoolhouse.

160

desks, the portrait of George Washington, the Palmer Method samples of the alphabet.

In their places Capt. George Earl III (U.S.N.-ret.) has placed sporting prints, a rack of gleaming rifles and shotguns, comfortable furniture, books, and a silver service. It has the looks of a British country gentleman's drawing room, not the meeting place for youngsters ever restless for recess.

The home is a model of what can be done with imagination, getting the most from a one-room schoolhouse.

Former pupils would never recognize it. The original one room is now divided about in half. One room is a living room, twenty-four by fourteen feet, paneled in dark wood, and with a lifesize oil painting of Capt. Earl's great-great-grandfather. The other half of the house includes a finely equipped galley—that's kitchen to landlubbers—and dining area. There's an upstairs now with two bedrooms and a bath. The two outside privies are long gone, but there's an addition to the building, a small apartment, with a living-dining room, bedroom, and bath, giving both him and his guests—often his children and grandchildren—privacy and independence of action.

Earl, a retired Philadelphia banker, recalls how he bought the schoolhouse:

"Frank Sager, who lives in the big house up the road, owned it, along with most of the land around here. I was looking for a comfortable place. I sold my big house in Brownsville, where I

Former pupils wouldn't recognize this school.

needed roller skates to get around. I rented this from Frank. He has a bunch of kids. I was sure one of the girls would get married, then say, 'Daddy, can I have the schoolhouse?' and I'd be out on my ear. And it was just perfect for me. I finally talked Frank into selling it to me. That was after I'd been here about a year, I guess."

He and Frank discussed land, since this school, like most of that era, was built on a small plot of land, barely enough for the school, the two privies, and a small playground.

"When I first talked to Frank about buying the place and additional land, he said, 'How much do you want?'

"Well, I didn't know but I

161

didn't want some junk house—or any house for that matter—built across the road. I told him. He said, 'I'll make a deal with you. You give me first refusal on your house if you ever decide to sell. I'll put it in the deed that I won't build anything on that piece. Why don't you just buy the field here by your house?'

"So, I bought four acres. There's a fine spring at the edge of it. There was no need for me to buy much more inasmuch as I'm protected by the deed."

There's still one link with the past in the converted schoolhouse.

George points it out. "See that picture over there. Well, that was one class. Jean Myles—she has the long, golden curls—is now over seventy. All the Jenney boys who live around here attended this school."

Thick stone walls make this a solid schoolhouse. It is in Sudbury, was built in 1829, and has not yet been converted to a home, the fate of a similar schoolhouse in the same town.

162

Little changed on the outside, the former Charlotte village schoolhouse is now modern on the inside. The home of Reginald and Elizabeth Gignoux, the house has a two-story living room, and an open stairway leading to a balcony and second-floor bedrooms and storerooms. A ship's ladder leads to the glassed-in belfry with a magnificent view of Lake Champlain, and both the Green Mountains and the Adirondacks.

SCHOOLS EVERYWHERE

Vermont once had nearly 2,500 school districts, and usually each had a one-room schoolhouse.

As an example, Weston, when it had a population of fewer than 1,000, had more than twenty one-roomers.

Why so many? Travel conditions were often difficult; main highways were muddy in the spring. Winter brought low temperatures and blizzards. Even buttonpocketed school board members didn't want six-year-olds walking far under such conditions.

Today only nine of the little schools are still being used. Some of the buildings still remain, not yet claimed for other uses. Real estate agents in rural areas often know where they are, and whether they can be bought.

163

It's not surprising to find a schoolhouse in Vermont with a long history linked with children, then another history of families living in the schoolhouse, and each making changes to it. This North Ferrisburg schoolhouse was a school for about seventy-five years, and has been a residence for the past thirty years. Two schoolteachers, Mr. and Mrs. John Bourgoin, have lived there for the past eight years. The home features a large living room with an open stairway leading to upstairs bedrooms. The walls are lined with books, prints, and a large record collection. A wing was added. It houses a kitchen and dining room.

From Historic Church to Modern Home

Opportunities for converting churches to homes are often passed by, and for a variety of reasons. A practical one is that churches have high ceilings, and high ceilings mean huge cubic feet of airspace that must be heated before those at ground level are warmed.

But the opportunity is not always passed up.

When in 1959 the Baptist organization in Vermont put up for sale the brick church in Baptist Corners, East Charlotte, a local resident bought it. He paid $4,000, then sold off the pews and other salvagable items, and finally, about 1970, sold the building to a couple who converted the building to a home.

"It's pretty much the same as it was when we took over," said the present owner, Dr. T. Brock Ketcham, radiologist in the Medical Center of Vermont. He and his wife, Pat, a former X-ray technologist, have owned the house for three years. One of their moves has been to install an airtight stove, to provide much but not all of the heat.

The main inside portion is painted flat white, as is the twenty-foot high arched ceiling. The kitchen, with an open counter, is on a platform, and overlooks the living room.

Sliding glass doors lead to a sundeck overlooking flower beds and a productive vegetable garden.

164

A former church provides a gigantic living room.

Index